Write Your Non-Fiction Book in 3 Months

(in only 30 minutes per day!)

Brigitte van Tuijl

ISBN Paperback: 978-90-830654-8-9
ISBN e-book: 978-90-830654-9-6

Visit www.booksbybrigitte.com for more books by the author.
For additional gifts, visit www.bookfreebees.com

The information presented in this book can help you write your first draft in three months, but I can't guarantee you will finish your book in that time frame. Your outcome depends on the content and length of your book, the type of book you're writing and of course, your commitment and dedication to the actual work of writing your book.

The information provided in this book is designed to inspire, educate, motivate, and enlighten you on the subjects discussed. It's not meant as a substitute for professional coaching or other expert assistance. If such level of assistance is required, please seek the services of a competent professional or contact the author directly for one-to-one coaching options. The author assumes no liability for use of the information and exercises.

Copy editor: Kelly Urgan
Cover design: Susan D. Johnson

Also by Brigitte van Tuijl

*The Gap - bridge the space between where
you are and where you want to be*

*The Inner Minimalist - clear the clutter of your
mind for a simpler, quieter and happier life*

The Art of Divine Selfishness Series

*Book One: Unmute Your Life - break free from
fear & go for what you REALLY want*

*Book Two: The Art of Divine Selfishness - transform your
life, your business & the world by putting YOU first*

Books in Dutch

Ontdek Wat Je Écht Wilt En Maak Daar (Je) Werk Van

CONTENTS

Part Three: Practical Writing Tips

Part Four: Troubleshooting Fears and Obstacles

I've always known I wanted to be a writer. But I never knew what I wanted to write about until I started my coaching business in 2003. I realized I didn't want only to coach but to write books that inspired and supported people, too!

It took me a while to write my first book. I was afraid my writing wasn't good enough, and I didn't know enough about my topic. I feared being seen as an imposter and a fraud. I was terrified of making myself visible and dreaded the practicalities of publishing a book.

In 2008 I finally felt confident enough to write my first book, and I self-published *Ontdek Wat Je Écht Wilt En Maak Daar (Je) Werk Van*. It was accepted by a publisher one year later, and the book has sold thousands of copies since.

Writing that book only took me six weeks, so when I started my second book in 2011, I expected a similar journey. HA! That turned out to be a *very* different story. This time it took me NINE years to write and publish my book. During those years, I wrote eight different versions of *Unmute Your Life - break free from fear & go for what you REALLY want*. I wrote those different versions for different reasons. Once I rewrote the book because I changed my audience when I took my business global in 2011. Another time I rewrote it because I tried to cram four books into one. I rewrote it again because I changed my mind on some topics. I rewrote it several more times because I felt it simply wasn't THE book yet.

I wrote a lot. And when I wasn't writing, I was *learning about* writing, editing, self-publishing, marketing, and selling books.

In June 2020, the book was finally finished. I sent it to the designer and at that point, there was nothing for me to work on. So I decided to write my next book. I was determined to keep my writing momentum going this time and started writing not one but two books at the same time.

I finished the first draft of these books, *The Gap* and *The Art of Divine Selfishness*, within three months—I finished both of them in September 2020. In October I started writing books five and six: *The Inner Minimalist* and this book you're reading now. I finished those in three months, too.

I realized I could write four books in six months because of *everything* I had learned and experienced over the years. All the fears I had, all the times I felt stuck, all the times I *hated* writing and wondered if I'd ever finish my book . . . all this taught me so much! What also made a difference was my coaching experience, which helped me coach myself through my stuck points, just like I help my clients move through theirs, plus everything I learned about writing.

Over the years, I've seen many people struggle with their books. But that's unnecessary when you know where to start and how to work through your fears and doubts. I helped clients write and publish their books and helped them save a lot of hassle and time. That's why I wrote this book: so you can benefit from my experience and expertise and finish your manuscript!

You'll learn how to turn your idea into a finished first draft. If you follow the steps and actually *write* thirty minutes a day, five days a week, for three months straight, you can finish your first draft in that time. You absolutely can!

I dedicated most of this book to mindset, overcoming obstacles and fears, and necessary prep work before you write. The reason for the emphasis on mindset is that the *writing* itself *is not* the hardest part of writing a book. The biggest challenge you have to deal with are the thoughts your mind throws at you.

Writing non-fiction is putting your content on paper in an orderly fashion. That's really all it is. Some people write better than others, but when you give your book your undivided attention AND hire a good editor, you're capable of delivering a good book. Only your fears and doubts make writing hard!

But fears don't have to stop you. I overcame my own massive fears, *and* I've been helping my clients do the same for almost two decades now. The tools, tips, and exercises in this book will help you move through doubts and write your book, too!

Part One helps you thoroughly prepare yourself. **Don't skip this part!!!** Going through the steps there sets you up for a successful and enjoyable writing journey. And it improves your book, too!

Part Two helps you embrace a positive mindset that makes working on your book easier and more fun.

Part Three gives you practical writing tips. Finally, Part Four helps you overcome obstacles and fears you might run into during your writing journey.

This book gives you what you need to start *and* finish your first draft. All you have to do is sit down, follow the steps . . . and write. And before you know it, your book will be done!

Happy writing!

Love,
Brigitte

WHY MOST PEOPLE NEVER WRITE THEIR BOOK (BUT YOU WILL!)

Many people want to write a book. But there are more people who *want* to write a book than people who actually *do*.

Some don't write it because they never start. Some never finish. Some don't start because they don't know *how* to write a book. Others don't because they're too scared.

Finishing your book takes dedication. Courage. And work! There's no getting around it: you can only finish your book when you sit your ass down and write. Not once, not twice, but as often as it takes until your book is done.

Not everyone has it in them to write—and publish—a book. Not because some people are born writers and others are not. (Even though some people are definitely born to write.)

Not because some are more talented than others. (Even though that's true, too.) But because some people overcome their fears and do what it takes to write their book. Others don't.

If you dream of writing a book, you have what it takes to do it. This dream didn't come to you for no reason! You may need some help. You may need to be shown how and where to start, or how to move through feeling stuck and face your fears. That's what you'll find in this book. Read it, follow the action steps, and WRITE. And before you know it, you'll hold your own book in your hands!

REASONS TO WRITE A BOOK

You probably already decided to write a book, or you wouldn't be reading this. But maybe you're not 100% sure yet. Maybe you wonder if it'll be worth your time and effort. I can tell you from personal experience, it is. So let me give you my top five reasons for writing a book. These should give you extra motivation to get on with your book!

Reason One: An immense feeling of satisfaction and accomplishment
It feels incredible to hold your book in your hands. It takes your self-confidence up a couple of notches. It feels amazing to realize that YOU MADE THIS! One moment this book was just an idea, the next it's an actual physical thing that others can enjoy. How cool is that?!

Reason Two: A book establishes you as an expert
If you run a business, this is very helpful. When people see you as an expert, it makes it easier for them to decide to work with you or purchase something from you.

Reason Three: A book helps you grow your business
A book gives people the opportunity to get to know you and your work. When they like what they read, you'll be the first person they come to when they want to learn more.

Your book can also function as a business card and a marketing tool. A book is great for creating publicity opportunities.

Reason Four: A book helps you make a difference

You only have to write it once, and then it can positively impact people for years to come. Once it's done, it doesn't cost you any extra time! (Besides the time to promote your book, but that doesn't have to be laborious.)

Reason Five: You can offer great value at a super affordable price

You can give fantastic value at a price everyone can afford, including people who can't afford your other offers. Don't be afraid to give too much or worry that people won't buy your services or other offers anymore!

My first book, *Ontdek Wat Je Écht Wilt En Maak Daar (Je) Werk Van*, describes the EXACT steps I took my clients through to find out what their dream job was. Many career coaches used my book to take *their* clients through this process, too. But this NEVER led to fewer clients for me. On the contrary!

One reason for this is that not everyone can implement information on their own. People often need accountability, motivation, encouragement, and support to move through the steps and potential obstacles. Another reason is the one I mentioned above: when people like your book and approach, the first person they turn to is you.

To this day, people sometimes inquire if I can help them find out what their dream job is—even though it's clearly stated on my website that I no longer offer career coaching. Not bad for a book that was published in 2008 and I haven't promoted since 2011, right?

The primary reason for me to write books, however, is that I can't *not* do it. Writing is in my blood and my bones. I'm born to write and I've known that since I was a kid. It's my purpose, my calling, my joy.

I have a deep inner drive to write, and I LOVE it. The five reasons I mention above are nice bonuses, but I'd write even if no one would read it and it didn't make me any money. Writing is an essential part of who I am.

You may have different reasons to write your book. You may already know what they are or have no idea. Either way, it's good to know your deeper motivations. That's one of the things you'll explore in Part One. **Start there.** The preparations in Part One make your writing journey much easier and will vastly improve your book!

PART ONE
BEFORE YOU START WRITING

INTRODUCTION TO PART ONE

You'd think that writing a book starts with writing. But it doesn't. It starts with *thorough preparation*. This part of the book takes you through it.

Don't skip this step because you're itching to write. Reading through the following chapters and answering the questions sets you up for an easier writing journey. It also improves the quality of your book!

Answering all questions helps you shape the content of your book, and it prevents your writing from going all over the place.

Exploring why writing your book matters to you will help you finish the book. Starting can be easy, but finishing can be harder. Some days your words flow with ease, other times it feels more like pulling teeth. Knowing the deeper motivation behind the desire to write your book will pull you through those harder moments.

Grab your notebook and dive into the next chapters. Answering the questions is fun and will serve you along the way.

Enjoy!

ACTION STEPS

Step One: Decide and commit

Decide to write your book. Commit to it. *Wanting* to write a book is one thing. *Doing* it is another. Just reading this book won't magically lead to a finished manuscript. If you're serious about your book, commit to it now. Write the following statement, or something similar in your own words, in your Book Folder (see step two):

*I'm excited to write my book, and I commit
to doing what it takes to finish it!*

Step Two: Create a Book Folder

Take a binder, notebook, or folder to save all your notes in one place. It can also be a document on your computer. It doesn't matter which option you choose. Whatever you pick, I'll refer to it as your Book Folder from now on.

My favorite is a physical folder. It's easy to put handwritten notes in it. I keep everything that has to do with my book in that folder, including for example my to-do list and ideas for marketing and promotion.

Step Three: Schedule

Turn your commitment into action. Take out your schedule / planner / diary and reserve thirty minutes per day, five days a week, for the next three months. During that time, you work on your book. And yes, this *includes* answering the questions in the next chapters. If you spend over thirty minutes, that's fine. If you have less time available, that's okay. As long as you consistently work on your book, you'll get it done!

Step Four: Pick Your Book

What book will you write? Maybe you have a bunch of ideas to choose from. If so, pick the one that excites you most.

If you're not sure yet, take a moment to feel into it. What would you like to write about? What ideas or topics speak to you?

YOU

Answering the following questions helps you find your deeper motivation for writing your book. The answers clarify why your book *truly* matters to you. Your answers will fire you up and help you start *and* finish your book. Reading through your answers brings back your excitement and motivation during the times when writing feels harder.

There are no wrong answers to the following questions. So don't judge, criticize, or censor anything that comes up.

Set aside some time when you won't be disturbed to answer the following questions and write down everything that comes to you. The numbered questions are what you need to answer, and the questions that follow are prompts to help you answer it.

1. Why do you want to write a book at all?

    Is it something you always dreamed about? Is it something you feel you have to do? Whatever reason(s) you have is perfect!

2. Why do you want to write THIS book?

    Why do you want to write about this topic? Why now?

3. Why should you write it?

    Why are *you* the perfect person to write this book? What makes it obvious that you should write about this topic? Think about your interests, experiences and personal story. Think about what fascinates you.

4. What will it feel like to have finished your book?

     Close your eyes for a moment and imagine that your book is published. What do you feel? What comes up when you think about this? How will you feel differently compared to how you feel now?

5. How will you transform and grow as a result of writing your book?

     What will you learn? How will you change? How will writing your book help you grow or heal? Anything else writing your book might bring you?

6. How will your business transform as a result of writing your book?

     What difference will your book make for your business? How could your business benefit from your book?

7. What difference will your book make for your reader?

     What will reading your book bring them? How will they feel? How will they change? What will they learn? What will become possible for them?

     For this question, write down whatever comes up. You can't be certain that your reader will experience the benefits you think of, and you don't have to be certain! Your answers are *your* idea of what *might* be possible for your reader. Your answers help ignite your passion—you're not writing sales copy and no one has to know your answers.

8. What difference does your book make for the world?

     How could the world transform as a result of your book? Set aside any thoughts of being arrogant and don't censor yourself!

No one will read your answer, so don't worry about how strange, megalomaniac, or unbelievable your answers sound. Answering this question helps you find an even deeper layer of purpose for writing your book.

9. Who do you need to be to write your book?

    What do you need to believe? What do you need to do or stop doing? Who is the version of you who successfully publishes a book? What does she look and act like?

10. How can you be that successful writer now (and always)?

    If you act like a successful writer now, what does that look like? What would you do? What would you NOT do? What would you wear, eat, believe or think?

    Write down your answers and act on them. Repeat daily.

My answers and why I share them

Maybe answering these questions is easy for you. But coaching clients for over two decades taught me that exploring your deeper dreams, motives, and desires can be hard sometimes. Some answers can scare you or make you feel uncomfortable. Sometimes dreams and desires can trigger feelings of guilt or shame: Who am I to dream this big? How arrogant of me to think my book could change the world!

As a result, you may censor your answers. You think you don't know what you want or you come up with answers you deem acceptable—but they don't represent your *true* desires and therefore don't light you up. *That's* the primary purpose of answering the questions in these first chapters. It would be a shame if you went through the entire process but you repressed your true answers.

For that reason, I'll share my own answers to all the questions. Seeing my responses might inspire you or help you feel that there's nothing wrong with your answers (or you!). Reading my answers can help you give yourself permission to feel what you feel and to want what you want, without apologizing or shaming yourself for it. If my answers aren't helpful or you don't need them, just skip this part here and in the following chapters.

These are my answers for this book, *Write Your Non-Fiction Book in 3 Months*. I typed the answers over from my Book Folder and only edited them for grammar and spelling to give you a real and uncensored look inside my head. ;-)

1. Why do I want to write a book at all?

    It's in my blood! I'm born to write and publish books. I've known this forever.

2. Why do I want to write THIS book?

    Because I've struggled SO MUCH with writing books myself. With my first book it took me a while before I felt courageous enough to even start writing. I had to conquer so many fears! With my second book it took me nine years to publish it. That process took me through a lot of emotions, doubts and fears as well. Thanks to those experiences, I learned more than anyone I know about moving through blocks and obstacles that are specifically related to writing books. It also taught me how much easier (and quicker!) writing a book can be. I successfully helped some of my private clients birth their books. I want more people to benefit from my expertise.

3. Why should I write it?

    My unique experience and knowledge: my writing journey (both struggles and successes) combined with my expertise as a master coach specialized in breakthroughs and realizing true dreams.

4. What will it feel like to have finished my book?

Great! Not the intense feeling of relief and accomplishment I felt with my previous books. This is my sixth, so it's starting to feel normal. But still: amazing! The idea that I'm *finally* writing and publishing multiple books after knowing this was my path for most of my life feels incredible! It also makes me feel grateful and humble.

5. How will I transform and grow as a result of writing my book?

I think it will make me feel even more like a real, grown-up writer. I mean, six books and counting! Plus, it's a book about writing books. That takes away the last niggles of doubts about being a genuine writer.

6. How will my business transform as a result of writing my book?

I don't know if it will really *transform* my business because I already have multiple books out. Maybe more books will change how others look at me or my business? Maybe people will see me as a writer first and a coach second, instead of the other way around like it's been for years. And maybe my business will seem more like a business based on books instead of a business based on coaching, as it has been for years. (Which, I realize as I write this down, is something I've been dreaming about since . . . 2010? A business based on books! And now it finally is! Oh wow, that's a big transformation and the fulfillment of an even bigger dream. Yay! Extra happy now!) Also, it adds an extra stream of revenue to my business. That's always nice. :-)

7. What difference will my book make for the reader?

It will make it easier for them to write their book. They'll be so relieved to see that they're not the only one who has fears and doubts about writing. They'll be happy to see that their fears are normal and even happier to learn how they can move through them! Also, when they follow the steps and instructions, this will shorten their writing journey. They'll feel good about the fact that they've (finally) started writing, especially when they know that most people who dream of writing books never even start! And if they sit their ass down and actually do the work, they *can* have a finished first draft in three months!

8. What difference does my book make for the world?

There are SO MANY amazing books that never see the light of day. So much wisdom that's never shared, so much knowledge that could benefit so many but reaches so few. When I look at my own clients and see how much beauty and value they have to share . . . what a gift it would be to the world if their expertise reached a much bigger audience! If everyone who's here to heal and change the world wrote a book that shared their healing, inspiration, and love . . . imagine that! Books change the world!

9. Who do I need to be to write my book?

Who I already am. The most authentic, real, powerful version of me. The true writer that I'm born to be and always was.

10. How can I be that successful writer now (and always)?

By showing up and working on my book daily until it's finished. By promoting the crap out of this book (and all of them). In my own way, as always with everything, but still: don't keep those books a secret and don't shy away from marketing and promoting them. Just write, publish, promote, and repeat that same cycle always. Remember: I'm born to write and I want to positively impact millions of readers all across the world!

ACTION STEP

Answer the questions
Answer the questions in this chapter and save them in your Book Folder.

YOUR READER

Who is your reader? It helps to have an image of your ideal reader in mind when you write. Your marketing becomes easier, too. When you know your reader, you know how to speak to them and show them why they need your book.

Your ideal reader can be a real or imaginary person. Every book has a different ideal reader, because every book has a different topic. Focus on your ideal reader for the book you're writing *now*. For your next book, answer the questions again.

You may not know the answer to every question, and not every question will be relevant for your book. Different questions can also generate the same or similar answers. It doesn't matter. Just write down what comes up.

1. Who is your ideal reader?

    What kind of person is it? Describe their character, lifestyle, way of being, how they make a living—anything that comes to mind.

2. Why does your reader pick up your book?

    What attracts them to it? What is it they want? What is it they REALLY want? What's their secret dream or desire?

3. What do they already know about the topic of your book?

   Are they complete newbies or experts? Have they learned or read about your topic before? How eager are they to learn even more about it? Why?

4. What obstacles (if any!) do they experience regarding the topic of your book?

   Where do they get stuck? What is it they can't seem to do? How is this a problem for them? What does this problem cost them, not just in terms of money, but also in loss of energy, time, or happiness?

5. What questions do they have about the topic of your book?

   What do they worry about? What do they want to know? What answers and information are they looking for? If *you* needed this book, what would you want to know? What questions would you have?

6. What do your readers dream of when it comes to the topic of your book?

   What do they desire? What do they want to change or experience? If they could wave a magic wand and see their dream come true, what would they wish for?

7. What do they need to know about the topic of your book?

   What's important for your reader to understand, feel, experience or do? What do they need to know to solve their issue?

8. What do you want your reader to take away from your book?

   What will they know, understand, feel, experience or be able to do after they read your book?

9. What has changed for them as a result of reading your book? What's different? How does this benefit them?

10. What's the name of your ideal reader?

Now that you've gotten to know your reader(s) in more detail, you can give them a name. Maybe you know someone in real life or you come up with an imaginary ideal reader. Name them. This can make it easier to write your book, because you can imagine yourself writing it for this specific person. Often, that's easier than writing it for an anonymous reader. (Don't worry if you can't come up with a name for your ideal reader. Not everyone finds this helpful. Me, for instance. I skip this step because it doesn't work for me. But I include it here because I know it works wonders for others!)

***

My Answers

(Skip this part if it's not helpful for you. See *Chapter 1: You* for the reasons I share my answers.)

1. Who is my ideal reader?

A super cool, driven person who wants to make a positive difference in the world. They have something to say about something they care about, and they want to share that message with more people because they know it can help others. They feel that putting their knowledge in a book would be a great way to share their message. They're basically the same as my ideal client for my online programs and coaching, coupled with the desire to write a book.

2. Why does my reader pick up this book?

Because they want to write a book! Their secret desire? For that book to be a bestseller. To positively impact others with their book. Maybe even to change the world! They'd also love it if their book brings in extra money (or maybe even makes them rich). Also, writing a book in three months in only thirty minutes per day sounds doable and attractive to them.

3.   What do they already know about the topic of this book?

They're completely new at writing a book and don't know anything about it. Or they have some idea of how it works, but they can't seem to start writing. Or they started but got stuck.

Maybe they already published a book but found little joy in writing it and wonder if there's an easier way to write their next book(s).

4.   What obstacles (if any!) do they experience regarding the topic of this book?

My readers don't know where to start or they get stuck while writing. Fears and doubts get in the way. They don't know how to determine what needs to be in the book. They're afraid their book will fail and / or they're afraid it will succeed. Writing doesn't feel joyful because their inner critic keeps telling them they suck or their writing sucks. They start when they feel good about their book and stop when they feel bad about it—they think feeling bad is a sign to stop because they don't know about the creative cycle. (I'll explain what that is later on in the book.)

5.   What questions do they have about the topic of this book?

They want to know how to move past being stuck, or how to move past their fears. Also, they want to know how to move forward when finishing their book seems to take forever. They want to feel motivated to keep writing and need inspiration to keep moving forward.

6.   What do they dream of when it comes to the topic of this book?

They want to help people. They want to change the world! Also, they want to finally *write* their book instead of only dream or talk about doing that. Maybe they dream of their book getting rave reviews and / or being a massive bestseller. Maybe they dream of their book changing lives and getting emails from readers sharing their love for the book. Maybe they dream about starting a movement and changing the world.

7.   What do they need to know about the topic of this book?

How it works to write a book / how to prepare before you start writing / how to create an outline / all the mindset stuff: how to deal with all the doubts & fears that come up. Some practical writing tips and inspiration to keep moving forward.

8.   What do I want my reader to take away from this book?

That they are more than capable to write their book!! I want them to feel confident about that. I want them to feel excited about their book. I want them to feel that they can do this, that there's enough space for their book. I want them to at least start writing and it would be the coolest thing if they actually finish their first draft in three months with the help of my book!

9.   What has changed for them as a result of reading this book?

They went from being stuck to unstuck. Also, they started writing!

10.   What's the name of your ideal reader?

As I mentioned above, I always skip the last question about giving your ideal reader a name because it doesn't work for me.

ACTION STEPS

Step One

Answer the questions and keep them in your Book Folder.

Step Two

Name your ideal reader, unless you're like me and this doesn't feel helpful.

YOUR BOOK

Now it's time to think about your book. Answer the following questions to clarify what you want your book to do for you. Write down everything that comes to mind. If nothing comes up, don't worry about it. Something may come to you later and if not, that's no problem at all.

1. What would you like your book to do for you?

    For example you can say: I want to be seen as an expert or grow my impact. Or I want to learn more about this topic.

2. What would you like your book to do for your business?

    For example: I want to grow my email list, bring in extra income or generate extra publicity.

3. Anything else you'd like your book to do?

    For example: I'd like to educate people or break a taboo.

4. Anything else comes to mind when you think about your book?

    Write down whatever comes up exactly as it comes up, even if it doesn't seem realistic or related to the book at all. You never know where your random ideas may lead you! I can't tell you how often my crazy concepts turned into a masterclass, a blog, or a chapter in a book. I also used my ideas in my marketing or book launches.

Tip

Keep all ideas in your Book Folder. In every stage of working on your book, ideas will come. You never know what you can use them for.

My Answers

(Skip this part if it's not helpful for you. See *Chapter 1: You* for the reasons I share my answers.)

1. What would I like this book to do for me?

    I'm not really sure. Maybe to improve my writing skills?

2. What would I like this book to do for my business?

    Reach people I'm not reaching with my other books yet. Grow my business.

3. Anything else I would like my book to do?

    I hope it inspires people who dream about writing a book to actually write it instead of only think about writing it.

4. else comes to mind when I think about my book?

    Not really. I'm just excited to write it!

ACTION STEPS

Step One

Answer the questions and keep them in your Book Folder.

Step Two

Review your answers from time to time. This keeps you motivated to finish your book.

YOUR INTENTION

Intentions are a powerful manifesting tool. Clear intentions help you consciously choose how you want to feel, act, BE, and show up.

When you write down intentions, you'll automatically start taking the actions that will help you write your book. That's because intentions help you consciously direct your energy, focus, and attention on what you want (instead of on what you *don't* want).

Writing intentions is easy. All you have to do is imagine what you'd love to feel and experience and write it out *as if it's already so.* Use present tense and first person.

I'll give you an example of my intentions after giving you some ideas on what you can include in your intention. For example:

- How you choose to show up during your writing journey
- How you choose to feel about writing your book
- How you want to act
- What you choose to focus on
- How you will grow and transform through writing your book
- What you'll learn
- And anything else you can think of

Here's an example of the intention I wrote for my upcoming book *The Happy Hermit - how to thrive as an introvert entrepreneur:*

> I'm looking forward to writing this book! It's so much fun to work on. I enjoy writing every single day. It's easy to sit down and write for thirty minutes. Time flies by, and I love every second! The inspiration I need comes to me abundantly and easily. The words flow out of me without me having to think about it. I finish the first draft quickly and editing is going rapidly. It's such a breeze! I love every second of working on the book and every phase of the publishing and promotion process. It all comes to me easily and I enjoy every step!

It doesn't matter what your intention looks like or how long it is, as long as you pay attention to these three things.

1. Write your intention in the first person.
2. Write it as if it's already so. Either use present tense ("I love writing my book! It's so easy and fun!") or past tense, as if you've already accomplished it ("I loved writing my book! I'm in awe at how easy and fun it was. I feel deeply fulfilled now that I can hold my book in my hands, and I'm excited for what the book will bring me next!")
3. Your intention feels fantastic. When you read it, you feel happy!

ACTION STEP

Write your intention(s) for your book and put them in your Book Folder.

OUTLINE AND STRUCTURE

An outline is the blueprint for your book. It helps you organize your topics and ideas so you know where you're going and what to write about. This makes writing easier and faster.

Once your outline is done, you can start writing your book, chapter by chapter. Your outline WILL change along the way, though! It's merely a starting point. New topics can come up while you write. You may add or delete chapters or reorganize the structure of your book along the way.

Still, having an outline is crucial. Writing *with* an outline is like driving to an address in a city you've never visited before and taking a map with you that shows you the way. Writing *without* an outline is like driving to that address without a map, without even knowing which city you need to go to.

Having an outline improves your book and makes writing it easier. Here's how to create it.

Step One: Make a list of topics

Here are two ways to make a list of topics that belong in your book.

1. View your book as the answer to a question. What is that question? What do people need to know to find the answer? What do they need to do, let go of, or understand to find the answer? Write down every topic that comes to mind.

For example, the question this book answers is: how can you write a good book in a reasonable amount of time? The chapters in this book are the things people need to know to answer those questions.

2. Look at the overall promise or topic of the book. What does your reader need to know, understand, and be able to do based on this promise? What do you want them to take away from the book? Write down every topic that comes to mind.

    For example, the overall promise of this book is that you're able to write your first draft in three months in only thirty minutes per day. Each chapter is a part of what you need to know or do to make that happen.

If your idea for your book is still very broad, now is a great time to narrow it down. Let's say you chose to write a book about finding your dream job. Topics you can think of are:

- How to find out what your dream job looks like
- How to create a good résumé
- How to write a great cover letter
- How to negotiate your salary
- How to make a good first impression
- How to land your first job
- How to find a job when you're over sixty
- How to turn your current job into your dream job

When you look at this list, it's clear these topics are for different audiences (people over sixty are probably not about to land their first job). It's also clear that there are too many topics to address in one book. Clarifying what your dream job looks like is a book in itself!

Based on this list, you can decide which topic to focus on first. That's the book you'll write. You can then make a list of topics that should be addressed in that book.

You can also decide to write a series of books on the overarching topic of finding your dream job. Start with one book and focus on the others next.

Step Two: Organize your topics

Write each topic on an index card or sticky note and put them in order. Keep moving them around until the order makes sense. Does it look complete? Do you need to add another topic? Can you put several topics together? Can you delete a topic?

Step Three: Fine-tune your structure

Each topic is a chapter in your book. With that in mind, look at your topics. Describe, in one or two sentences, what you should address in each chapter. When you do this, you can see if two or more topics belong in one chapter, or if you should divide one topic into two or more chapters.

Once your list of chapters seems complete, see if you need to rearrange the order. You can also see if it makes sense to divide the book into several sections or parts. For this book, for example, it made sense to divide the book into four different parts.

You don't have to divide your book into different sections, though, that's just ONE way to structure your book.* You can also put all chapters in a logical order or find another way that makes sense for your book.

---

* For more examples of book possible book structures to inspire you to create your book, sign up for free bonuses at www.bookfreebees.com

Remember: Your outline and structure will probably change along the way. Whatever you come up with now is enough to write your first draft!

ACTION STEP

Create your outline

Brainstorm a list of topics for your book. Don't write off any ideas yet! Some ideas may not end up in your book, but you may use them somewhere else. In another book, for example. Or you can write a blog post about it.

Once you feel your list is complete, go over steps two and three and create the outline and structure of your book. Put it in your Book Folder.

Now you're ready for the next step: to create a (working) title for your book. Already have one? Skip *Chapter 6: Title Tips,* and *Chapter 7: Create Your Title,* and go to *Chapter 8: Talk to Your Book.* You can always return to those chapters if you need help finalizing your title.

TITLE TIPS

Don't worry, you don't have to come up with your final title right this second. It often takes a while before you find the "perfect" title, anyway. Sometimes it only falls into place after your book is finished!

At least come up with a *working title*, though. That makes your book feel more real. Here are some tips to help you come up with an attractive title.

Tip One: Don't use jargon

Unless you're writing an academic paper, avoid jargon like the plague. Your title should speak to your ideal reader so they're attracted to your book.

Tip Two: Be clear

Does your title clearly state what your book is about? Does it sound appealing to your ideal reader? *Write Your Non-Fiction Book in 3 Months (in only 30 minutes per day!)* is crystal clear. A reader knows what it's about and is instantly interested—or not. I could also have called it *How to Enjoy Your Writing Journey More*. That would also fit the content of this book, but it's less clear and not as attractive.

Tip Three: Speak to a dream, desire, pain, benefit, or result of reading the book

Your book is the answer to someone's question. It helps them ease a pain or achieve something they dream of. They want to learn or accomplish something. If you speak to your reader's desire in the title, they'll be drawn to your book.

Here are some examples of fictitious titles* that I came up with to show you how you can address people's dreams in a book title.

1. *How to Lose 25 Pounds in 5 Months (Without Eating Less or Exercising More)*

    This speaks to several desires at once. To lose weight. To lose it in a relatively short time. To lose weight without being hungry or spending more time in the gym.

2. *Your Dream Job – How to Land the Job of Your Dreams Within 6 Months (In Every Economy!)*

    Who (besides entrepreneurs) doesn't want to land their dream job? In only six months? And it's even possible in a recession?! That sounds amazing.

3. *The Money Tree – The Effortless Way to Grow Your Income*

    More money! Without effort! If this book existed, it would sell like hot cakes.

What pain or dream does your book speak to? What can people achieve or let go of by reading your book? How could you capture that in your title and subtitle?

---

* I checked: none of these titles exist now. If you find a book with one of these titles later, the author was probably inspired by this book. :-)

Tip Four: Use a title and subtitle

You don't have to, but most non-fiction books do. Your subtitle clarifies what the book is about and usually makes a promise or speaks to a desire.

Pro Tip: Use keywords in your subtitle

Keywords are search terms people use to search for information or books about your topic. You can find those keywords by typing in a word and watching how Amazon or Google autofill it. When you put those terms in your subtitle, your book will show up in people's searches!

I haven't actually used this tip myself, by the way. I didn't check relevant keywords for any of my titles. I might for my eighth book, though. I mean, it's a great tip. :-)

Tip Five: Be unique

Google your title to make sure it's unique. Strangely enough, book titles aren't protected by copyright. (The content of books is!) So technically, you *could* use a book title that's already in use. But why would you do that? It's confusing. And wouldn't you rather have an original title?

Pro Tip: Purchase the domain name the moment you settle on your title

I purchase two domain names for each of my books.

One domain name redirects to the book page on my website. For this book, that's www.bookin3months.com, for example. Other domain names that were closer to the title of the book were already taken.

The other domain name redirects to a sales page for an online program that takes readers deeper into the contents of the book. For this book, that's www.3monthbook.com. The program covers additional topics that aren't addressed in this book, like editing, marketing, self-publishing, how your book helps you grow your business, and more.

I used to also purchase a domain name that redirects to a page where you can sign up for gifts and bonuses. But I felt that I was getting too many domain names, so now you can find the book bonuses for all my books on one page, www.bookfreebees.com.

You don't have to purchase two or three domain names like I do. You also don't need to offer free bonuses or create an additional online program. If you're looking for ways to use your book to grow your business, these are just a few options.

Tip Six: Easy to remember

You want people to remember your title. It should be easy for them to go to a bookstore or online retailer and find your book. It's likely people will remember *The Money Tree*. It's less likely people will remember *The Metaphysical Principles of Abundance and Creation.** (I made up that title too.)

Tip Seven: Keep it short (or not)

You often hear it's important to keep your title short. I disagree. It's nice if your title is only a couple of words, but it's not required. As long as it's clear and memorable, you're good to go.

Tip Eight: Easy to pronounce

When someone is excited about your book and wants to recommend it to a friend, it helps if they don't trip over their tongue trying to pronounce it.

Tip Nine: Attention grabbing

The best way to check if your title gets noticed is to test it. First, be honest about your title. How does it sound? Imagine you didn't write it and hear the title for the first time. What would be your first impression? Does it sound like a book you want to read? Or does it sound boring? If so, CHANGE IT. When *you* think the title's bland, others will think so, too.

The second way to test it is to share your title *with your potential readers*, and see how they respond. It's nice when your parents think your title is brilliant, but are they representative of your ideal readers? Is their judgment clouded by love and pride?

If your clients are your ideal readers, ask them. If your friends represent your ideal readers, ask them. If not, find a group on Facebook (either a group of potential ideal readers OR a group of fellow writers) and ask them. Does the title appeal to them? What do they think your book is about? This tells you if your title is well chosen or if you should tweak it.

Extra Tip

Once you know your working title, you can create a mock cover, print it, and hang it on your wall. It's inspiring to look at it while you write! Search for "free book templates," fill in your name and title, and your temporary cover is finished.

Once I know the title of my book, I send it to my designer. When the cover design is ready, I have it printed and laminated. I hang it on the wall of my Creation Station (aka my office, but I don't use that word because it sounds boring and smells like work). It makes me happy to look at my cover collection. It's very inspiring and helps me stay motivated to finish my book!

ACTION STEP

Move on to the next chapter and start crafting your title. Use the tips in this chapter to come up with good ideas.

CREATE YOUR TITLE

Step One: Brainstorm

Come up with fifty (yes, fifty!) titles. I know, that's a lot! You can come up with them in several sittings, though.

Start by writing down as many titles as you can come up with. Put your list away and add more titles after a couple of days. Let your list rest again and add more titles later.

The reason to come up with fifty titles is that you have to dig deep and get creative to reach that number. This brings you ideas you'd never have thought of if you only came up with ten titles.

Once you thought of fifty titles, put your list away and don't look at it again for at least one week.

Step Two: Fine-tune

Come back to your list and read through it. Narrow it down to fifteen or fewer options. Don't throw the other titles away. You may use one of them for a blog post or in your sales copy later.

Try different combinations of titles with different subtitles. This may lead to your title. If not, put your list away again. Focus on writing your book. Sometimes you need to finish your first draft before the title can fall into place. Stay open to receive inspiration. If you get a brainwave, add it to your list.

Experiment with your ideas again later. Repeat until you find a title that feels like a winner. Use the tips in this chapter to find your title.

Ask for help if you get stuck. Preferably from another author or someone with insights on (copy)writing.

Step Three: Test your title (optional!)

If you wonder if your title works, ask for feedback from your ideal readers. Set up a poll on social media or email your list and ask people to vote for their favorite title.

Always go with your gut. If you feel confident about your title, there's no need to test it. (I never do. I sometimes ask for feedback from copywriting-savvy friends and colleagues, but usually I just *know* my title when I see it.)

Step Four: Before you decide on your final title

I already mentioned this: double-check to make sure your title isn't already in use. You *can* legally use it, but why would you? It's confusing and gives the impression that your book isn't original.

Don't use names or phrases that are trademarked or protected by copyright. You can't use a line from a song, for example, without getting permission.

You can't refer to other books or authors. You can't use a title like *The Book About Meditation Oprah Winfrey Wishes She Read 20 Years Ago* for example.

Read your title out loud, or let someone else say it to you. Does it sound good? Is it easy to pronounce? What else do you notice?

TIPS TO COME UP WITH TITLE IDEAS

Tip One: Check bestseller titles

Look at bestsellers in your genre and see which titles speak to you. Explore what you like about them. Look at the structure of these titles and what format they follow. See if you can come up with something similar for your book.

Play with your title. See if you can fit it in the format of five bestseller titles and if this sparks new ideas. You can find bestseller titles by searching for "non-fiction bestsellers." For example, when I typed in "non-fiction bestsellers" on Amazon, this title came up: *The Simple Heart Cure: The 90-Day Program to Stop and Reverse Heart Disease.*

If I experiment with that format for this book, I come up with these.

The Simple Book Guide: The 90-Day Program to Write Your Book
The Simple Book Guide: Finish Your First Draft in 90 Days
Writing Books Made Easy: How to Write Your First Draft in 90 Days
The Easy Way to Write a Book: From Idea to First Draft in 90 Days

Tip Two: Use a quote or idea from your book
In my book *The Inner Minimalist—clear the clutter of your mind for a simpler, quieter and happier life,* I use the phrase "crappy thoughts, crappy life; happy thoughts, happy life."

I could have played with that and turned it into a book title, for example:

Happy Thoughts, Happy Life - How to Turn Your Thoughts from Crappy to Happy and Improve Your Life
From a Crappy Life to a Happy Life - How Changing Your Thoughts Changes Your Life!

Go over your manuscript and see if you can find a phrase or idea you can turn into a title.

Tip Three: Play with words or expressions
Make up a word. (Make sure your subtitle clarifies what the book is about! You don't want to alienate readers by using a term that means

nothing to them.) Or take a common expression and play with it. The expression "money doesn't grow on trees" could turn into this title:

Your Own Money Tree - 5 Easy Steps to Make All the Money You Could Ever Need.

I made up this title, so this book doesn't exist. At least, not at the time I'm writing this!

Tip Four: What's the essence of your book?

If you have to explain what your book is about in ONE sentence, what would you say? See if that brings you some ideas. For example, if I described what this book is about in one sentence, it would be "how to write a non-fiction book." That's pretty close to the title already.

Tip Five: Name your audience

Who is your ideal reader? Can you address them in your title? For example, *Fifty Easy, Healthy Recipes for Busy Parents (That Your Kids Will LOVE!)*

I made this title up, too. It does not exist at the time of writing this book.

Tip Six: Be unique

What sets your book apart? Can you play with that? Perhaps your book gives soup recipes made of ingredients people normally don't make soup with, like apples, grapes, or chocolate. Your title could be *Strange Soups - Fifty Recipes for Delicious Soups Made With Unusual Ingredients You Find in Your Kitchen!* This book doesn't exist either; I made it up.

Tip Seven: Search

Search Google for "blog title formulas." Play with some of these formulas. Not all blog title formulas work for book titles, but they might bring you some fresh ideas.

Coming up with the perfect title is a mysterious process. Finding the title for my book *Unmute Your Life—break free from fear & go for what you REALLY want* took forever. I brainstormed at least 100 titles, and it took me months to come up with my final choice. Sometimes I wondered if I'd *ever* find it!

The titles of my other books came to me with more ease. The title for this book was clear after brainstorming only three or four options. The title for my book *The Gap - bridge the space between where you are and where you want to be* came to me at the same time I received the idea for the book. The same thing happened with *The Inner Minimalist*. The title for *The Art of Divine Selfishness - transform your life, your business & the world by putting YOU first* took more work because I found it hard to create the subtitle.

I don't know why some titles come to me with more ease than others. What I *do* know is that it's important to write down ALL your brainwaves. Even when you think an idea won't work, you might actually love it later.

TALK TO YOUR BOOK

Everything is energy. You, your thoughts, the table, trees, your dreams, this book, *your* book, inspiration, ideas . . . it's ALL energy. Your book already exists in the energy, it just hasn't materialized yet. It needs your effort to make it real so people can read it. But it already exists on some level! This means you can connect with its energy and ask it to support you in different ways.

You can ask your book to help you find the right words and bring you the inspiration you need. You can ask it who your ideal readers are or which topics to include in your book. You can ask input for the structure or how to best promote it. You can ask your book *everything* you want to know or need help with!

I know this may sound strange but give it a go, anyway. Even when you don't believe you can connect with your book, doing this exercise can *still* bring you wonderful insights. Who knows? And who cares if these insights came from your book or you made them up yourself? If the information is helpful, that's great!

Here's how you can talk with your book.

Make sure you won't be disturbed for the next fifteen minutes. Have a pen and paper nearby. Take a moment to relax, get quiet and turn inward. Close your eyes. Breathe in and out deeply until you feel calmer. Relax your eyes, eyebrows, mouth and jaws. Drop your shoulders.

Once you feel more relaxed, invite your book to connect and communicate with you. Use whatever words feel natural. You can formally invite your book to show up or simply think, *Hey there, book, come talk to me, please!*

Open your eyes and write down a question. Any question. Next, write down *everything* that comes up, *exactly* as it comes up, without censoring it, thinking about it, or questioning it.

Then write down another question. Again, write down everything that comes up. Ask as many questions as you like. Here are some examples of questions you can ask.

- What topics do I need to address in the book?
- What does my ideal reader need to know about the topic of this book?
- What are some good ideas to launch this book?
- What ideas do you have for marketing the book?
- What helps me to write my book?
- What ideas do you have for the title?
- What must I include in this chapter?

Important Guidelines

Take a moment to relax, turn inward, and get quiet first. This makes it easier to focus and let answers come up.

Get out of your own way. Step aside and let in anything that wants to come through. Put *all* words onto paper and *do not* think about, label, judge, censor, or question them.

Don't worry if this is weird or if you feel you're making it all up. Who cares if you imagine it or you actually chat with your book? If you can use some of the information that comes through, who cares where it came from?

I talk to my books all the time. I talk to everything, really. It's all energy, remember? You can connect and communicate with everything.

I talk to my car, my laptop, my plants, birds, trees, my spiritual team, and even myself sometimes. ;-)

If this doesn't speak to you, skip this step. You can write your book without it. But if you're curious or this intrigues you? Try it! You have nothing to lose, right? Besides, who knows where inspiration *really* comes from? Did you ever say something and wonder how you knew that? Did you ever get an idea and wonder how you came up with it? You can't *really* be sure where anything you think comes from, can you?

You can also connect with your book before you start your thirty-minute writing session. Connect to your work, as I described above, and ask your book to guide, inspire, and support you while you write. Then, write.

ACTION STEP

Talk to your book if and when this feels good. Save your notes in your Book Folder.

YOU'RE READY TO WRITE!

Your preparations are done. You know your reader and why you write. You have a working title and an outline for your book. You're ready for your next step, which is to start writing!

Maybe you can't wait to start. Or maybe you dread writing or feel scared. If so, know that it's normal. It's scary to start a book. This is my sixth book, and I notice the same pattern every time. When I first get the idea for a book, I'm excited! Creating an outline feels great and I love the book already. But when it's time to write, I'm less confident. I'm not sure about my outline, doubt if the idea for the book is worthwhile, doubt if I'm the right person to write it—even when I felt certain of that before.

These doubts don't stop me, because I know uncertainty about yourself or your book is part of the creation process. (You can read more about that in Part Two, *Chapter 7: The Creative Cycle*). So I start anyway. I sit down five days a week and write for thirty minutes each time. But I don't enjoy it at first. For the first two or three weeks, it takes discipline to write daily. Then, somehow, something shifts. I look forward to writing. It feels inspired and fun. I thoroughly enjoy the process of creating! I continue to write for thirty minutes each day until the first draft is done. Some days I love it, other days I feel so-so about writing. Some days I make excellent progress, other days I'm certain I'll delete everything I wrote later. (And sometimes I do!) Several times throughout writing, editing and publishing the book, I go from feeling excited and feeling good about my book to feeling it's a bunch of crap and it'll NEVER be a good book.

It can be scary to begin and scary to finish. Sometimes writing feels easy and sometimes it's difficult. That's normal. It's all part of the process. So if you feel scared now, know that this is NOT a sign to wait or give up on your book. On the contrary. It's a sign that you're ready to write. Your book wants to come to life. Your fears and doubts are part of birthing a book.

So start writing. Start anywhere: write the introduction or a random chapter. It doesn't matter where you start. *Just start.*

If you need more guidance on how to start, read Part Three, *Chapter 1: From Outline to Writing*. Read the mindset tips in Part Two if you need more motivation. If fears, doubts or other blocks come up, look through the topics in Part Four. These chapters help you troubleshoot obstacles. Also, check out the practical writing tips in Part Three. These can help you as well.

Start writing now, even when you have questions or fears to work through. Write for thirty minutes daily, five days a week. Repeat until your book is finished. It's really that simple. Not always easy, though! That's why a large part of this book is about thorough preparation, mindset, and troubleshooting. But it IS this simple.

Happy writing!

ACTION STEP

Start writing. Repeat daily. You're ready for it, even when you don't feel ready yet!

PART TWO
THE WRITING MINDSET

INTRODUCTION TO PART TWO

Your *thoughts* are what make writing easy or hard. The way you *think* about writing and your book determines how you *feel* about it.

The following chapters give you perspectives that help you feel good (or at least better) about writing. The tips and tools make your writing journey easier and more fun.

If at any point you don't feel good about working on your book, come back to these chapters and read through the topics that speak to you. Or go over the chapters in Part Four to dismantle whatever block or fear is in your way.

Writing itself is *never* hard. It's *always* what you *think* about writing that determines your experience and how you feel. The following chapters help set your mind right.

FIRST DRAFT

The MOST important thing to remember when you start to write is that you're writing your *first draft*. Your concept. The first version of what will become your finished book.

When you let that idea sink in, this gives you so much freedom! What you write doesn't have to be perfect or polished. It doesn't even have to be *good*.

ALL you have to do in this moment is put words on paper. That's it. Your first draft is *not* what your published book will look like. Once this draft is ready you'll edit, rewrite, and polish. You'll delete and add sentences, paragraphs or even entire chapters.

Your first draft is the entrance to your finished product. Without this first version, you'll never be able to publish your book.

Putting ANY words on paper is more important than the quality of your writing. It doesn't matter if it's bad. It doesn't matter if a chapter feels unfinished or if your wording isn't clear. It doesn't matter if your writing is clunky or if you overuse certain words. You'll fix it later.

But you can only improve what's already written. Without a rough draft, it's impossible to publish a book. Writing your first draft is a step in the process of publishing your book. Nothing more and nothing less.

All you have to focus on now is to write your first draft. It may turn out good, but it's fine if it sucks. You'll clean it up later. If you don't know how to improve something, your editor will.

CHAPTER 2

ALLOW YOURSELF TO FAIL

Now you know you're writing only a first draft, and it's okay if that version stinks. I invite you to take it one step further and allow yourself to fail: allow yourself to write the worst book in the world. Give yourself permission never to publish it.

This doesn't mean that you set out to write a crap book. It also doesn't mean your book will never see the light of day.

What it means is that by giving yourself permission to mess up your manuscript, you remove the pressure. Of course you want to write a good book! So do I. But your expectations and hopes for your book can be a burden. They can put so much stress on you that you choke on your words before they have a chance to come out.

If you want your book to sell well, make you and your family proud, and change the lives of your readers, these motivations *can* inspire you to write. They can also paralyze you.

It's okay to have expectations and hopes for your book. It's okay to set intentions and strive for success. But when they cripple you? When that stops you from writing or turns it into an agonizing experience? Set yourself free. **Give yourself permission to let your book be a massive failure.** I'm serious. It works!

I start all my books intending to deliver the best book I can. I do what I can to make that happen. AND . . . I'm okay with never publishing it. I'm fine with throwing some or ALL of what I wrote away.

(Which is what I did several times with my book *Unmute Your Life,* as you read in the introduction.) It frees me to know it's okay to screw things up. No one ever needs to know! Freedom!!

CHAPTER 3

FEEL FREE TO BREAK THE RULES

You may not be consciously aware of any rules about writing. But I guarantee you that your mind is filled with them! Some stem from what you learned in school, others from reading books.

Give yourself permission to break the rules. **There's really *only* one rule to follow: to deliver a readable book.** (And you don't even have to do that! If you want to write an unreadable book, you're free to do so.)

Even when you don't break any rules, knowing you *can* feels freeing and makes writing more enjoyable. It's your book and you can do whatever you want with it!

I remember reading Stephen King's book *On Writing: A Memoir of the Craft*. I read the first foreword, the second foreword, and the third foreword . . . and I was so excited about that. It liberated me! I always assumed a book could only have ONE introduction or foreword. Reading those three forewords made me realize I could do *whatever the hell I wanted* with my book. Which is weird, because that's the way I've looked at my business and my life for as long as I can remember. But with writing, I felt restrained by sets of rules I didn't even know influenced me!

All these restrictions evaporated just by seeing Stephen King doing it differently. That very moment I gave myself permission to write my book *exactly* as I wanted to.

In the end I did nothing unique or out of the ordinary with *Unmute Your Life* (or any of the other books I wrote so far). But knowing I *could* if I wanted to, changed everything for me!

Give yourself permission to do whatever you like with your book. It's yours, you're the boss, and you decide!

CHAPTER 4

SEE YOUR BOOK AS ALREADY DONE

Imagine what it will feel like to have finished writing your book. It's done and you're a published author! Close your eyes and take a moment to feel it. See yourself holding your book. Think about what you'd say to your best friend when your book is done. How would telling her that make you feel?

Remember that feeling. More importantly: think of your book as already done from now on. It's already here. It's already real.

Act as the person who has already published her book. *Write* as the person who has already published her book. Walk like her. Eat your pie like her. Dress like her, think like her, and talk like her.

One of the most powerful manifesting tools is acting and feeling as if what you dream about is already real.

Pro Tip

Use this mindset for everything you desire. Be the one who already has what you want *now*, and whatever it is you want can unfold for you quicker and easier.

Acting like a person who has already published her book gives you more confidence. You trust yourself more. Acting like your book is already finished positively impacts you. Someone who *tries* to write a book might not invest in an editor, or work on her book consistently until it's finished. But someone who *acts like she has already published her book*? She hires a good editor. She finds a designer who creates an attractive cover. She writes every day until it's done, whether or not she feels like writing.

This may not make sense to you yet. Try it anyway. Here's how you do that. Every morning, take a moment to remember what it feels like to have published your book. Close your eyes and take a minute to immerse yourself in this feeling. Do this daily before you write. Take actions and make decisions from the perspective that your book is already done.

Need more help? Ask yourself this question: What would I do today if I knew it's a given that I'll publish my book? What decision would I make if I fully trusted my book will be published? What would I let go of when I *know* I will finish my book? Act on the answers you get. Repeat daily.

FOCUS ON YOUR PROGRESS

Sometimes it can feel like it takes forever to finish your manuscript. There's so much to do and think about! If you focus on *finishing* your book, you're constantly affirming that it's *not* ready yet. That can make you feel disappointed, overwhelmed, impatient or rushed. Focusing on everything that's *not* done yet can make you doubt yourself and what you do. Will you ever finish? Are you doing enough? Are you doing the right things?

Thoughts like these aren't helpful. They make writing harder and take away your joy. **Shift your focus to your progress**. Look at how far you've come instead of at what you still need to do. Even if all you write is one sentence, that's still one sentence more than you started with! Every single word you write brings you closer to finishing your book.

If you like, you can celebrate your progress regularly. You have every reason to! You started writing, which is great. Most people who dream of writing a book don't even start, remember? You prepared, made an outline, and came up with a working title. You wrote a couple of sentences. That's progress! Lao Tzu said centuries ago that a journey of a thousand miles begins with a single step. You took that step. You're on your way! If that isn't worthy of a celebration, I don't know what is. :-)

You're making progress. All you have to do is keep going and before you know it, your book will be done.

MAKE YOURSELF AVAILABLE
FOR INSPIRATION

Don't make the mistake of thinking that inspiration comes first and writing comes second.

It *can* work that way but more often, it works the other way around: you sit down to write and inspiration follows.

Inspiration comes when you make yourself available for it. That's why W. Somerset Maugham said, "I write only when inspiration strikes. Fortunately, it strikes every morning at nine o'clock sharp."

Don't wait for inspiration to come to you. When you do, it could take forever to finish your book! (IF you finish it at all.)

You're not at inspiration's mercy. **Inspiration is all around you, always—you only have to receive it.** You receive it by writing. You receive it by *expecting* inspiration to come to you at the perfect time. Not a moment too soon, not a moment too late. You receive it by paying more attention to the inspiration you already get.

When I started writing monthly newsletters in 2005, I was afraid I'd run out of topics to write about after a couple of months. I had ideas for four articles, but what would I write about after that? Would I be able to come up with a new idea every month? How long could that possibly last? I was *seriously* concerned.

Turned out that I had more than enough to write about. After a while I started writing a weekly newsletter, too, which meant I wrote five articles per month. The inspiration kept coming. *It never stopped.* The main reason for that ongoing flow of ideas was that I *committed* to writing. I vowed to write five articles per month whether or not I felt like writing. Whether or not I felt inspired. I wrote something, sent it to my list and posted it on my website five times per month. Even when I wasn't certain if what I wrote was any good. No matter what happened or how I felt, I wrote five articles monthly!

I changed the number of articles I wrote over the years. For a while, I wrote a new blog every day, week in week out. Then I scaled back to two or three blogs per week. It varies now. But I ALWAYS write. And because of that, I ALWAYS have inspiration. In fact, I have more inspiration than I know what to do with! I have over fifteen ideas for books on my book-ideas list. I don't know if I'll ever get around to writing any of them, because I keep getting new ideas for books that want to be written first. I'm *drenched* in inspiration. That was NOT the case when I first started writing! That only happened because I kept writing, with or without inspiration. I never gave up. I also changed my mindset. I DECIDED that inspiration would always flow to me. I started EXPECTING that to happen even before it actually happened! I stopped waiting for inspiration to come and made myself available for it by writing as much as I could.

As a result, I experience an abundance of ideas now. I know inspiration is available to me ALWAYS, in greater amounts than I'll ever need or can use. I can count on that and trust it completely.

Inspiration is abundantly available for you, too! Don't worry that you'll end up with less inspiration when you use the inspiration you receive. The opposite is true: the more inspiration you use, the more inspiration you get!

THE CREATIVE CYCLE

When you write a book you go through the creative cycle multiple times, sometimes even daily. This cycle starts with excitement. You have an idea for a book and you love it! You feel good about the idea and your ability to write. You're doing it! This is fun!

Then the excitement wears off. Your level of joy gradually drops. With every drop, you have more doubts until you end up on the other end of the spectrum, where you think your book sucks, your writing sucks and *you* suck, too. You're certain your book is crap and no one will like it.

This cycle is completely normal. Chances are you'll go through it more than once. The best thing to do is to accept that going through this creative rollercoaster is a normal part of writing a book (or creating anything, really!) It's NOT a sign to stop, and it's NOT a sign that something is wrong with you, your book, or your writing. It's a sign that you're creating something from nothing and you're entering unknown territory. You put your soul and inner world on paper to share with the world, and you have no idea what will happen next.

When I first got the idea for my book *The Gap,* I absolutely LOVED it. But once I started writing it, I was convinced it was utter crap that no one would want to read. The *only* reason I finished the first draft is because my intuition told me I should. If I'd listened to my rational mind, I wouldn't have finished it. My mind was only feeding me negative thoughts. But after I let the manuscript rest for a couple of weeks and I read it again with fresh eyes, I was pleasantly surprised. It wasn't half bad! I decided it was good enough to publish and that's what I did. If I'd listened to my doubts, I'd never have done that!

I go through the creative cycle multiple times with *all* my books and *every* online program I create. My extremes are *extreme.* When I'm excited about an idea, I feel like it's the best idea the world has *ever* seen, and I'm certain my book will be an instant bestseller. How could it not?! When I'm on the other end of the spectrum, I'm certain I'm writing the *worst* book *ever* written in the history of the world.

Eventually I land with a more balanced state of mind. ;-) At the end, I'm happy with and proud of my book. I'm certain I did my best and feel good about that. Then, I don't think about it anymore. I create something new and go through the same cycle again.

I learned to not let this up-and-down process bother or distract me. All I listen to is my inner drive and knowing that a book wants to be written by me. And that's what I do. **None of my extreme thoughts are true.** My books aren't the best books ever written, and they're not the worst ones the world has ever seen either.

Besides, it's irrelevant what *I* think of the quality of my book. I can't look at it objectively, and it's not my job to judge my writing. My job is to write and publish books and deliver the best work I'm capable of. So that's what I do.

Your book is probably not the best or the worst book in the world. Your only job is to write your book as best you can. Your inner voices can shout all they want, but you don't have to listen to them. Ignore them. One moment they think you're doing well, the next they think you're delivering crap.

Just keep writing. All you have to focus on now is finishing your first draft. You can fix everything that needs fixing later. An editor can help you with that.

GET OUT OF YOUR WAY

You write best when you get out of your own way. When you're open, words and inspiration can flow to you and through you freely. **The more you get out of the way, the better your writing will be and the more you can enjoy the process.**

How can you step aside and let writing be easy? You can only do that when you're completely present. Present in this moment, present in your body, present with what you're doing: writing. When you're present, you can enter a state of flow. You're not forcing anything to happen, you *allow* it to happen. You *allow* the words to flow onto paper.

Writing can be a type of meditation. You become one with your book, your words, this moment, and your breath. It's a great place to be!

How do you get there? How do you get out of your own way? The following tips help. Practice applying one or more of them and see what happens.

PRO TIP: live your WHOLE LIFE in this state of presence and awareness. It makes everything better!!

Tip One: Be present

Bring your attention to this moment and your body. Do that by breathing in and out deeper and slower. Put one hand on your belly and feel it rise and fall with your breath. Or do this breathing exercise. Inhale for four counts, hold your breath for four counts, and breathe out for four counts. Repeat until you feel calm.

Another way to get present is to consciously focus on one sense at a time. Close your eyes. Focus on what you can hear in the distance and nearby. Register all sounds without labeling or judging them. Focus on what you can see with your eyes closed. Then focus on everything you can smell. After that, notice what you taste in your mouth. Finally, pay attention to how your body feels. Do you feel any aches, pains, or tingles? How does the air feel on your skin? Are you warm or cold?

Don't *think* about any of it. Don't judge, label, or criticize it. Just notice and observe. This brings your attention to the present moment and your body.

Tip Two: Become grounded

When you do the breathing exercises above to become present, you usually also become grounded. The more grounded you are, the easier it is to be present in this moment and in your writing. If you don't feel present in your body yet, jump up and down a couple of times. Dance a bit or do some physical exercises. Doing that will help you land in your body. You'll feel calmer, clearer and stronger, which also helps you feel more confident about your writing.

Tip Three: No distractions

When you're ready to write, turn off your phone and all notifications, close your browser and your email, and tell the people around you to leave you alone until you're done.

Tip Four: Set your mind right

All you do for the next thirty minutes is WRITE. You don't answer emails. You don't think about dinner. You don't think about tomorrow, yesterday, what's on your to-do list or what movie you'll watch later. You don't do *anything* besides writing. Don't think about anything else and don't even think about the entire book. All your focus is on the chapter you're working on and the sentence you're writing. Everything else can wait.

After thirty minutes, you can look at what requires your attention next. But for now? YOU WRITE. When your mind draws a blank you let it draw a blank, but you DO NOT use that as an excuse to answer an email or send a text. Nope. You stay where you are until the next word comes up.

If no words come up, you can write about *that*. Write how it makes you feel to not know what to write. Type it out of your system. In the middle of your chapter, even. It's fine. You can take it out later.

Just. Write. Down. Words.

You can polish, edit, rewrite, or delete anything you write later. You can't edit an empty page. So. Just. Write.

Tip Five: Don't judge your writing

Type words for thirty minutes. That's it. Don't judge the quality or the quantity of your writing. Just write. It doesn't matter if it's "good" or "bad." It doesn't matter if you write one word or a thousand. Right now, your only job is to put words on paper, and that's what you do.

Tip Six: Open and allow

Set your intention to be open to what wants to come through you, whatever it is, exactly as it is. Allow the words to come out, even when you think they're weird, stupid, or bad. Allow inspiration to take you by the hand and guide you. Allow your book to be what it wants to be. Allow yourself to be, to breathe, to let this moment be this moment, to let the words be the words, to write without judging or overthinking. Allow it all. How? By saying out loud that you're open and will allow inspiration to work through you. By reading this paragraph out loud. Or by simply thinking, *Yes, I'm open and I allow words to flow to me and through me. I'll write them all down and that's all I have to do now.*

Tip Seven: Be with what is

That's another form of being present. You just ARE. Yes, you're writing. But while you write, things happen: your back aches. Outside, you hear sirens. Your neighbor puts on loud music. You notice that you're hungry or are desperate for another cup of coffee.

Thoughts and experiences like these can distract you OR you can just BE with them. This means that you notice it, but you don't *act* on or give attention to any of it. You only notice what you feel and what goes on. And then you let go. You don't get up to make a sandwich. You register that you're hungry and then put it aside. It is what it is, and it can wait for another thirty minutes. When you don't think about, act on, react to, fight or resist *any* of your thoughts and experiences, you can continue to write even if you're hungry or annoyed.

PART THREE

PRACTICAL WRITING TIPS

INTRODUCTION TO PART THREE

You prepared yourself for writing by going through the steps in Part One. You finished your outline and you can get started!

The next chapter helps you cross the bridge from your outline to actually *writing*. Read through it and get cracking!

Use the other tips in Part Three if you need them. The most important thing you can do now is sit down and write five days a week until your book is finished.

Happy writing!

CHAPTER 1

FROM OUTLINE TO WRITING

Your outline is done. You have a list of topics that go into your book. Each topic is one chapter.

Maybe you also came up with a structure for your book. By structure I mean that the topics are bundled together in different parts that each have one overarching theme. (Like the four parts of this book.)

Other elements can be included in your book, too. For example, an introduction and / or a foreword, a table of contents, the copyright page, etc.*** Add these to your list of topics that go into the book. Create a new folder in Word, or whatever program you use to write your book in. I work with Scrivener, for example. (When you sign up for bonus gifts, in a short video you receive I show you how I set up the outline for my book in Scrivener and then start writing.***)

Write one chapter after another and tick them off of your list.

Here are two additional tips.

Tip One: Start anywhere

You don't have to write your book from beginning to end. You can start anywhere. I usually write the introduction last, for example. When I

*** You receive an overview of the elements that are often part of non-fiction books when you sign up for bonus gifts at www.bookfreebees.com

I also show you how I go from outline to writing my book using the Scrivener writing software. You don't need that program, but watching how I work with it might bring you some practical ideas for writing your book. Plus, you can compare this finished book with the outline I started it with. ;-)

write it first I usually end up rewriting it, anyway. That's because at the beginning, I'm not sure how the book will turn out. Somehow that blocks me from writing the introduction.

I usually start writing whatever chapter calls me first. I look at my outline and pick a topic that catches my eye. If nothing jumps out, I start with the first chapter.

If there's a particular topic or chapter that you feel like writing, ALWAYS start there!! It calls you because the inspiration for that chapter is ready to flow. Always work *with* your inspiration, never against it. It's okay if you jump back and forth through your book.

Tip Two: Don't number your chapters
Once you start to edit, you might rename, reorder, or delete chapters. It saves you time and hassle if you number your chapters only at the end, when you're certain about the order of the chapters.

BE CONSISTENT

Don't wait until you have time to write. MAKE time to write. Make it your priority and write regularly. Preferably five days per week. Write for thirty minutes each day until your book is done. If you don't have thirty minutes per day, write for twenty minutes. If you can't find twenty minutes, write for fifteen, ten or even five minutes. Write regularly until you finish your book.

There will always be other things you must do. The timing will never feel perfect. The best way—the ONLY way—to get your book done is to keep writing. Be consistent and write regularly. If you don't, it takes much longer to write your book. You lose your momentum. Writing takes longer, becomes harder and less joyful when you have to find your rhythm every time.

I learned this lesson while writing my second book, *Unmute Your Life*. A lot of factors contributed to that journey taking nine years, as I wrote in the introduction. But I also noticed that it took me a long time to get back into the book after each writing break. Now that I write my books in thirty minutes per day until they're finished, I notice how much better that feels. **You build momentum when you write daily.** At first, getting into the habit of writing five days per week isn't easy. I don't feel like writing, I procrastinate, and thirty minutes seem to take forever. For the first two or three weeks, I have to gently force myself to write. But then, suddenly, there's a turning point. Writing becomes part of my daily routine. I don't question it, I don't procrastinate, I just automatically sit down and write. Words flow with more ease, thirty minutes fly by, and there's no stress or hassle around writing. I just *do* it.

That's the power of being consistent, of getting into a routine, of making a habit. It saves you a lot of time and energy.

WHEN YOU WRITE, YOU WRITE

When you write, you write. I already mentioned that this is *not* the time to edit or rewrite. You do that at the end, after you finish your first draft. The same goes for doing research or anything else that comes up while you write: do it later. Do it *after* you finished writing for the day, or when your manuscript is ready. Make a note in your manuscript or write your action on a separate to-do list. But whatever you do: do not let it interrupt your writing!

Every time you interrupt your writing, you break your flow. It takes a while to get back into it and this costs you precious time and energy.

Plus, editing is a different process than writing and uses different parts of your brain. Switching between these parts costs a lot of time and energy. It also makes it harder to focus on what you're doing.

When I write, I write, and I invite you to do the same. Ideas and questions come up while I write. I put them in my manuscript and highlight them. My manuscripts are filled with highlighted passages. I make notes of everything I need to check and random ideas that come up. I remind myself to find synonyms for overused words. I jot down ideas for bonus gifts I can offer.

I don't interrupt my writing flow for *anything*. Everything can wait until the thirty minutes are over. Edit, research, and figure things out later. It's more efficient and makes writing easier, too!

CHAPTER 4

DON'T READ WHAT YOU WROTE

After you finish your daily writing, you're done. If you feel inspired to write longer than thirty minutes, you're free to do that. But you don't have to.

At the end of the thirty minutes, if you haven't finished your chapter, just write "Pick it up from here" or" Start here." When you open your document tomorrow, that's where you start.

Close your document once you finish writing. Don't read what you wrote. When you do that, you'll be editing and rewriting before you know it, and you **don't do that until after you finish your first draft.**

SAVE YOUR MANUSCRIPT IN MULTIPLE PLACES

You don't want to press the wrong button and lose your book or something you just wrote. Make sure *nothing* gets lost, not even when your computer explodes or your house floods. Save your manuscript in multiple places, including in the cloud where you can access it from any computer.

I save my file in Scrivener, in Word, on an automatic back-up that's made daily AND in the cloud. It might be overkill, but this way I'm certain I'll lose nothing.

YOU DON'T KNOW WHAT TO WRITE

Sometimes you want to write and words won't come. When that happens, write how you feel and what you think. It can look something like this: I don't know what to write. I don't know where to start. I don't even know what I want to say about this chapter. Maybe I don't even want to keep it in the book. Do I want to write the book at all? Today, I'm not so sure.

Writing down your thoughts clears your mind and opens up your writing channel. The content for your chapter will soon follow. If it's not good enough, you polish it once you edit. If you wrote something that sucks, you delete or rewrite it later.

Everything is fixable. Just put words on paper, *any* words at all.

CHAPTER 7

ALWAYS BRING A NOTEBOOK OR YOUR PHONE

Inspiration can strike at any time, so it's smart to always have a notebook or your phone nearby. I guarantee you'll need it!

I often wake up with ideas for my books. When this happens, I email them to myself from my phone. I go back to sleep immediately after that.

I also get ideas while walking, shopping and, of course, in the shower. Did you know you can get special notebooks to hang on your bathroom wall? They're water resistant, so you can make notes while you shower!

I always have *something* with me to take notes on. Make sure you do that, too. That way you won't miss inspiration when it comes to you.

CHAPTER 8

TIPS TO STAY MOTIVATED

It's not always easy to stay motivated to finish your book. These tips help.

Tip One: Remind yourself of your WHY.
Look at the answers you gave to the questions in Part One. Remind yourself why you want to write your book. Why does it matter to you?

Look at the difference finishing the book will make for you and your business. Remind yourself what your book will bring your reader.

Tip Two: How will it feel?
Imagine how it will feel when you've finished your book. Revel in that feeling for a couple of seconds.

Tip Three: What feels better?
Ask yourself what feels better: to continue writing and finish your book, or to quit and never publish it?

Tip Four: Celebrate
Celebrate what you've already accomplished. Celebrate what you learned. Celebrate your progress. Celebrate the fact that you started and are on your way to finishing your book. Most people never start writing, so you're doing great!

Tip Five: Who do you want to be?

As I mentioned before: there are more people who dream of writing a book than people who actually do. Which group do you want to belong to? The eternal dreamers? Or the published authors?

Tip Six: Talk with your book

In Part One, *Chapter 8: Ask Your Book*, you learned how to communicate with your book. Do that now. Ask your book to inspire, guide, and support you. Ask your book if it has a message for you or how it can help you. Ask it anything you want and write down everything that comes to mind.

Tip Seven: External deadline

Sometimes it can help to have an external deadline: a promise you make to another. You can set an external deadline by putting the publication date of your book on your website, for example. Or post on social media that you're writing a book and when you expect to be done. Tell the people on your email list the same thing.

This tip *can* work wonders if all you need is a little nudge or push here and there. However, it can also backfire if your book needs more time. During the nine years it took to write and publish my book *Unmute Your Life*, I used this external deadline strategy a couple of times. I announced the book would be ready by a specific date several times—but it never was. No one cared about that, but *I* did. It made me feel like I failed and I should have done better. Missing my deadlines more than once also made me doubt myself. So I changed tactics and stopped talking about my book. I decided I wouldn't say another word until the book was with the editor and I was certain I'd publish it.

Now, I talk about my deadlines and expected publication dates again. It motivates me to write daily until I finish my book.

I'm willing to break all my deadlines, though. Quality is more important than speed! Setting deadlines keeps me connected to my book and helps me write daily. If deadlines have that same effect on you, set them. If not, forget about it. You don't need deadlines to finish your book!

PART FOUR
TROUBLESHOOTING FEARS
AND OBSTACLES

INTRODUCTION TO PART FOUR

The main reason people don't start or finish their book is that fears or obstacles stop them. That's why I address some common blocks and doubts in the following chapters.

If nothing bothers you now? Great! Keep doing what you're doing and skip this part of the book. You don't need it.

But if doubts and fears come up, come back to this section and look up your fear. If it's not addressed in one of these chapters, go to *Chapter 16: General Exercises to Deal with Fear,* and work with one of the exercises.

Fears don't have to stop you. They have no power over you; you have power over *them.* The following chapters show you how to handle your fears so they no longer hold you back.

CHAPTER

THE FEAR THAT YOUR WRITING
ISN'T GOOD ENOUGH

You don't have to be an excellent writer to write a valuable non-fiction book. A novel written by a so-so writer is a waste of trees. But when you write a book about how to create your own WordPress site or how to meditate, it doesn't really matter if you're a talented writer. The most important thing is that you're able to convey your message in a way people understand and that they can easily implement. You need to write coherently and efficiently, but your writing doesn't have to be poetic or beautiful. If you can address your topic in a way people can grasp, you can write a non-fiction book.

Over the years I read A LOT of non-fiction books that weren't written well. I read some business books that were so badly written it almost made me cry. If these books had been regular novels, I'd have thrown them out after reading the first one or two pages. But the *business content* was excellent. So overall, I enjoyed my reading experience and took a lot of value from these books.

You don't have to write as well as Toni Morrison, Alessandro Baricco, or Elizabeth Gilbert to write your non-fiction book. If you can string clear, understandable words together, you're good to go! Plus, practice and a good editor can vastly improve your writing.

Good writing starts with good thinking. If you're clear about your message, half the work is already done. That's another reason it's important to create an outline before you start to write. If you find it hard to write a chapter or wonder if your text is clear, think about exactly what you want to say. These questions help.

- What's the essence of this chapter? Describe it in one or two sentences.
- What do you want your reader to take away from this chapter?
- What do you want your reader to know or understand after reading this chapter?
- What's the main thing your reader needs to know about this chapter?

The answers to these questions help you find the right words and express your message clearly.

THE FEAR THAT NO ONE IS WAITING FOR YOUR BOOK

Many writers fear that no one will want their book, and this is a major reason people don't write their book. They look at books that are already published and wonder what they could possibly add to that. Everything has already been said!

I know how disheartening this can feel. I felt this way before I wrote my first book in 2008. A business coach told me I had to do market research first. "Figure out what sets your book apart from other books on the same topic," she said. "What makes your book different? Why would people want to read *your* book?"

I started my research and quickly regretted it. There were more books about my topic than I knew. Every book seemed even better than the next! Pretty soon, I had *no* idea what made my book different. On the contrary . . . I felt that there was no place for my book. Everything had already been said. There was nothing original about my work. Why bother?

But then I re-read Eckhart Tolle's book *The Power of Now: A Guide to Spiritual Enlightenment.* I read it for the first time in 2001. Every word resonated with me. But I didn't understand most of what I read. Which made reading the book both an amazing AND a frustrating experience. I *knew* what I had read was meaningful and profound. But because I didn't really understand it, I had no clue how to implement the book's wisdom.

Thankfully, the market for mindfulness books exploded after the success of *The Power of Now*. One book after the other appeared, and I devoured many of them. Some I liked, some I didn't. Some spoke to me, some didn't. But I was so fascinated with the topic that I kept on reading.

I can't remember how many books about mindfulness I read, but I know what happened when I re-read *The Power of Now* in 2008. I suddenly understood EVERY WORD. I knew what Tolle was talking about, and more importantly, I now *also* knew how to implement his wisdom!

This would NEVER have happened if those other writers hadn't written *their* books "because there are already so many books about mindfulness." Without those other books, I'd never have understood Tolle's message. I'd never have known how to be present. I'd never have made significant changes in my life if I hadn't read those other books.

This experience helped me see that it's important for there to be MANY books about the same topic. Different books speak to different readers. Every writer brings their own flavor, tone of voice, and perspective. Someone can learn something from your book they didn't understand before. Your perspective or example can bring someone an insight they didn't get from other books on the same topic.

No matter how saturated the market for a topic seems to be, there's ALWAYS space for YOUR book, too. What you say may have been said by thousands of others. But it hasn't been said by YOU. Your voice is still missing. There is plenty of space for your book!

Besides, you didn't get the idea for your book for no reason! When you're inspired to write a book, this means that there are already people out there who want to read it. That's how life works. Your book is the answer to another's question. The universe is smart like that. :-)

THE FEAR OF SHARING YOUR OPINIONS AND BELIEFS

It takes courage to write a book, present your opinions to the world, and ask money for it, too.

Know that there will be people who agree with you, and people who won't. It's impossible to write a book that everyone loves. Your book is not and cannot be for everyone. No matter what you say or how you say it: your message will never please everybody. And that's okay. It's neither your job nor your responsibility to make everybody happy. Your job is to write your book to the best of your ability, to be true to yourself and what you believe in, and to express that as best you can. Some people will love your book, some will think it's okay, some will dislike it, and most people will never even know your book exists.

People read *your* book to read *your* opinions, visions, and ideas. If you water those down, your book becomes bland. The blander your book becomes, the less it offers your readers.

Be true to yourself and put your heart, soul, knowledge and wisdom in your book. Then let it go. The moment your book is published, it's literally and figuratively out of your hands. It's anyone's book now. Every reader will read their own version of the book, depending on their worldview, perspective, dreams, fears, values, and beliefs.

This is not something to fear, this is something to celebrate! This frees you up to do your own thing, because you have NO control over how people will respond to your book. The only thing you have full control over is what you write and how you write it. What your reader will think and what your reader will or won't agree with is out of your hands. Hurray! You don't have to think about that. All you have to do is focus on your book.

Even when someone disagrees with you or dislikes your work, what harm can that do? How bad is that, *really*? It's not the end of the world, is it? It can feel that way for a moment, but I promise you the world won't end when someone doesn't like your book. For more tips on dealing with this, read the next chapter on the fear of criticism.

Remember, the only opinion that *really* matters is your own.

THE FEAR OF CRITICISM

What compliments and criticism have in common is that they're not about you. They're a reflection of something you inspire or trigger in another person, and they project their reaction onto you. This doesn't mean you can't graciously accept a compliment. It also doesn't mean you have to reject every critical remark about your work. There can be truth in compliments *and* critique.

The best way to deal with criticism is to learn from it (IF there's something to learn), and to reject and ignore all comments that are unhelpful, untrue, or disrespectful.

Don't take any of it personally. Compliments don't make you a better person, and criticism doesn't diminish your value. Remember to separate critique of your *work* from your *worth*.

The best thing is to do your best, be true to yourself, and write the book *you* want to write. Act in alignment with your values and integrity. Make your book the best you can and make sure you feel good about your work before you publish it. When you feel good about it, other people's opinions won't matter much anymore!

Remember that criticism often says more about the reader and their personal tastes than it does about your book. I remember receiving two reviews on my first book *Ontdek Wat Je Écht Wilt En Maak Daar (Je) Werk Van* on the same day. The first reader wasn't too thrilled about the number of quotes in the book. He felt there were too many. The second reader raved about the quotes: "It's one of the things I loved most about this book!" Same book, same amount of quotes. Different readers, different comments. In retrospect I think the first reader had a point. I went a little overboard with the number of quotes. :-)

When there's truth in feedback, learn from it. Other than that, let it go. Do the best you can and make sure you feel good about your book. When you do that, you never have to fear criticism. You don't need anyone's confirmation or compliments to prove that you're worthy or good enough. Both criticism and compliments don't define you. Feedback on your book has nothing to do with your value as a human being!

The only approval you need is your own. The opinion that matters most is your own. Don't let your fear of criticism stop you. Don't let your need for approval or compliments drive your behavior either. Write your book and publish it. You'll be fine, even *if* some people don't like it!

CHAPTER 5

THE FEAR THAT YOU DON'T KNOW ENOUGH

Your book reflects what you know NOW. You'll be capable of and know more later. But you don't write your book later. You write it now.

You know enough to write your book. But be mindful of the promise you make to your reader. If you promise more than you deliver, your reader will feel unsatisfied. If you make good on your promise, your job is done.

There's always more to know and more to learn. You'll never reach a point where you know absolutely everything there is to know about *any* topic.

Don't wait until you know more. Make your book the best you can make it with the knowledge you have today.

CHAPTER 6

THE FEAR THAT YOUR BOOK ISN'T GOOD ENOUGH

When you read through your finished manuscript, can you, in all honesty, say you did the best you could? Check it by answering these questions.

- Does the title of the book match the content? Do you deliver what the title promises?
- If applicable, did you check facts?
- If applicable, did you ask permission to use quotations?
- Did you take the time to thoroughly edit the book yourself?
- Did you hire a professional editor to improve your manuscript?
- Did you hire a professional designer to design the cover and / or design the interior? If not, are you ABSOLUTELY certain that your work looks professional?
- Did you do your best to deliver great value?
- Do you feel that you gave it your all?

If you answer these questions with *yes*, your book is good enough. If you answered one or more questions with *no*, address the issue and try again.

There may still be people who don't like your book or don't think it's good enough. You can't please everyone and you don't have to. As long as *you're* pleased with your book and you know you gave it your best shot, you're ready to publish it!

The reason people think they don't have time to write a book is because they think they need long stretches of time to do it. You don't. I write my books in thirty minutes per day. I understand that finding even that amount of time can be a stretch. If that's the case, see if you can write for twenty, fifteen or even ten minutes per day. **When you're consistent and write daily, five days a week, your book WILL get done!**

You can always find at least ten minutes to write. Even if that means you have to get up earlier or go to bed a bit later. That's what some of my clients do. You can also look at how you currently spend your time and see where you can squeeze in some writing. How much time do you spend scrolling through social media? How often do you check your email? Where else could you save time that you can spend on your book instead? Ask your soul and the universe to create extra time for you. You never know what clever solutions they will come up with.

Finally, look at how you spend your time—your life!—in general. Do you spend it on people and things that matter most to you? Do you spend time to pursue your dreams, including writing your book? If not, what are you waiting for? We all know that "one day" never comes . . .

CHAPTER 8

THE FEAR OF MAKING YOURSELF VISIBLE

This is a BIG and very common fear. I used to have it myself. Being visible scared me so much that I didn't have a website for my business for two years! I also didn't do *any* marketing or networking because that scared me too much. I overcame my fear ONLY because my business was suffering because of it. I wasn't able to make enough money and there were only two options left: to learn how to make myself visible and get clients OR to get a job. The latter was not an option for me. Going back to a job felt a million times worse than overcoming my fears around visibility, so I decided to overcome it, step by step.

First, I set up a website. Then I started writing a monthly newsletter and built an email list. I continued to write articles and after a couple of years I felt confident(ish) enough to write my first book.

What was the main thing that helped me get over my fear of being visible? It was that my dreams were bigger than my fear. The same is probably true for you. Go back to your preparations from Part One. Remind yourself of the reasons you want to write, your passion for your topic, your excitement for your book. Also remember that the *overwhelming* majority of people on this planet will never know about you or your book.

Read through your notes in your Book Folder. Look at the reasons you want to write your book and how your book will benefit you, your business, and your readers.

Finally, you can journal on these questions. How is *not* writing your book better than writing it? And how is writing it better than *not* writing it?

Answering these questions ignites the fire to help you finish your book. When your desire is bigger than your fear, there's no limit to what you're capable of!

PERFECTION PARALYSIS

There's nothing wrong with striving to write a brilliant book. But when perfectionism slows you down or stops you completely, it's time to deal with it.

Let's first look at some things that do NOT help so you can stop doing them.

- Telling yourself that "good enough is good enough."
- Telling yourself to stop being such a perfectionist.
- Saying it's okay to make mistakes.
- Reminding yourself that no one is perfect.

None of this helps because perfectionism isn't the issue.
Yes, you read that right. Perfectionism isn't the problem. On the contrary: it's the solution to an underlying problem! Perfectionism is your friend, trying to keep you safe and protect you from pain.

Here's how that works. Let's say you're afraid to publish your book. Perhaps because you're afraid to make yourself visible or because you fear criticism. Maybe you're afraid no one will be interested in your book and it will fail miserably. Or maybe you fear it will be an enormous success!

These fears can trigger so much anxiety that it is too scary to look at them. It feels too frightening to publish your book!

That's when your inner perfectionist jumps in. She slows you down. She helps you by stopping you from finishing your book. Because if you never finish your book . . . you'll never have to experience any of these fears!

Your inner perfectionist is smart. She gives you the illusion she's helping instead of sabotaging you. She tells you that you'll be safe when your book is flawless. She tells you that no one will hate or criticize your book when it's perfect.

At first you believe these thoughts. They make sense! Of course, it's important to deliver a perfect book. That's the best way to avoid criticism. And why would you settle for anything less than a perfect book?

But when your perfectionism stops your progress, it has nothing to do with the quality of your work. Your perfectionism is sabotaging your progress to keep you away from fears, pain, and failures.

The REAL issue is not your perfectionism, but a deeper fear your perfectionism is trying to protect you from. That fear is the problem, and the solution to your perfectionism is to address your fear. Examples of those deeper fears are: the fear that you're not good enough, the fear that your book will fail, or the fear to promote your book.

Often all you need to do is *look* at your fear and allow yourself to *feel* it. To *be with it* without labeling, judging or thinking about your angst. To feel it in your body and breathe through it, so the energy of fear can move through you.

Ask yourself what you fear or resist. What might happen when you publish your book? What might happen when you continue to write? What might go wrong? How might you get hurt?

Explore these questions with an open, curious mind. Don't judge anything that comes up. Just be curious to see what goes on inside you, because once you know what holds you back, you can shift it.

Write down whatever scares you. Chances are your worries are addressed in this part of the book. If not, go to the last chapter with general exercises to deal with fears.

CHAPTER 10
WHAT IF YOU CHANGE YOUR MIND?

Changing my mind is something I worried about when I self-published my first book. What if, in a couple of years, I'd change my opinion on something I wrote?

To solve that issue, I gave myself permission to change my mind. I decided the book could still have value for my readers, even if I had a change of heart on one of the topics in my book. I was also willing to change the manuscript and print new books if I that felt was necessary.

Turns out that it wasn't. A publisher published my book one year later, and I didn't want to make any changes then. I also didn't want to make changes for the second edition. When I look at the book now, I can see that I've outgrown it. I developed my writing voice and if I wrote that book today, it would be a different book. And that's okay. I made my book the best I could make it and that's all that matters. And it continues to have value for readers today.

Will I still love my books in five, ten, or fifteen years? I don't know. Will I still believe everything I wrote? I don't know. It doesn't matter. All that matters is that I do the best I can *now*. IF I no longer believe in one of my books, I'll know what to do then. I can take it out of publication, update it, or leave it as it is.

Give yourself permission to change your mind, to update your book, to rewrite it, or to take it out of publication later. You'll know what to do *if* this ever becomes an issue.

It's possible that you will outgrow your books. You change, learn, and mature, always. Your writing gets better with practice. But your book can still have value for others, even when you're no longer in love with it yourself.

Do your best work and give yourself permission to change your viewpoint later. It's okay to change your mind.

If you still feel uncertain, you can always put a disclaimer in your introduction or on your copyright page. You can add something like this: The content of this book represents what I, to the best of my knowledge and intent, now know and believe. I reserve the right to change my mind later.

CHAPTER 11 — WHAT TO DO IF YOU STOP WRITING

What should you do if you lose your routine and you don't write for days or weeks?

First, don't blame, shame, or guilt yourself. That's not helpful and doesn't change a thing. Sometimes resistance, life, or fear gets in the way. It happens. Sometimes, you actually *need* a break. Why? Because ideas need to percolate or you need a pause to find a fresh perspective. It's all good. Don't worry about it. It doesn't matter that you stopped writing, what matters is what you do next. Don't think about the time you weren't writing and focus on moving forward and not looking back.

If it's difficult to write, explore why. Is there something you fear? Is there something you are resisting? Is there a downside to finishing or publishing your book? What do you fear might go wrong when you continue to write?

Notice the answers that come up and address any fears or doubts. One of the chapters in this book can probably help you out.

Sometimes, however, you need a longer break. Now, it takes me three months (at most) to write the first draft of my book. But my second book *Unmute Your Life* took me nine years. The book wasn't ready before that. And neither was I. I needed to go through some transformations to *fully* embrace my destiny as someone who writes and publishes lots of books.

Yes, you can write a first draft in three months. Yes, the tools and tips I give you in this book help you do that. If fears and blocks are delaying your progress, you can shift them and keep writing, anyway.

But every book *also* takes as long as it takes. You, like me, may need time to heal or transform before you're ready to birth your book. Your book may need time or your potential readers may not be ready for it. Whatever the reason your progress stalls, you can trust the timing of your book. You can trust your process and path, and you can trust yourself.

If there's nothing you fear or there's nothing you're resisting, explore your motivation. Do you still want to write this book? Do you still love your topic? Look at the answers you gave in the first four chapters in Part One. Remind yourself of how good it feels to have finished your book. If you still desire to write your book, take a deep breath and start again.

If none of this helps, let it rest. Check in with your book now and then. You can get back to writing any time you want.

If you can't do this alone, get help. Hire a coach, join a writing group or writing program, or ask a fellow writer for support and write together. Whatever you do: don't give up. You CAN do this. Commit to yourself and your book, get support if you need it, and you'll get it done!

Don't worry, it won't have to take nine years like it did for me. And if it does? I *promise* you it'll be worth it. Those nine years were some of the most transformative, enriching, and empowering years of my life. It often sucked when I was in the middle of it, but I'm so grateful for the experience now!

HOW CAN YOU TELL WHEN YOUR BOOK IS DONE?

You can work on your book forever. There's always something you can change or improve. Always! That's why it's a good idea to set a deadline. For me, that deadline is the date I send my manuscript to my editor. I know I take three months to write the first draft. Then I let it rest for four weeks before I start the first round of self-edits. I go through at least five rounds of self-edits, and then I print the document to go over it one last time before I send it to my editor. I give myself eight weeks between finishing the first draft and sending the manuscript to my editor. That's how I calculate when my book is ready.

Once I start editing, I first read through the entire manuscript without making any edits. Reading the book in one sitting gives me a general overview of what still needs work. I also check if the book feels complete. If it doesn't, I explore why that is. What, if anything, is missing? What, if anything, can be deleted? My decision to add or delete something is always based on these principles:

- Does it improve the content of the book?
- Does it improve its readability?
- Is it necessary for the reader to know this in order to have the best possible reading experience?

Ask yourself the same questions, too. If you answer them honestly, you'll know when your manuscript is finished. You'll still need to edit it, but your first draft is done.

If you're still not sure if your book is finished, this usually has to do with fear of the next phase: publishing your book and presenting it to the world. Maybe you fear possible criticism, or you fear promoting your book, or you fear the book failing—or being a success!

Your book is done when you decide it is. When you feel it's ready, it's ready. When you decide it's complete, it's complete. Could you work on it longer? Always. Is it really necessary? If you did the best you could, no.

You can also read *Chapter 6: The Fear That Your Book Isn't Good Enough*. This gives you some extra questions to check if your manuscript is done and good enough.

MY BOOK SUCKS!

That's probably untrue. It's more likely that you're in the downward phase of the creative cycle. Read Part Two, *Chapter 7: The Creative Cycle*. It explains what that cycle looks like. We all go through it when we create. More than once!

Don't worry if you're at a stage where you doubt your book or yourself. It'll pass. Just keep writing and before you know it, you'll feel better.

If you feel doubtful for weeks on end, explore what's going on. Two things can be happening. One, your book needs extra love and attention. Go back to Part One and read through your answers. Does your outline still feel right? Did something shift along the way? Do you need to make structural changes in the book? Do you need to split the book into two books or do you need to broaden the scope of your book? Make the necessary changes. If you're not sure what needs to change, talk through your book with a coach or a friend. Preferably someone who knows about writing books or creating other types of content, like online programs, for example. Talking it through helps you see what (if anything) needs to change.

The other thing that might be going on is that a fear crept in, usually a fear connected to getting your book out into the world. Doubting the quality of your book is a way to make sure you don't have to address that fear. After all, if you don't publish your book, you don't have to face your fears of criticism or visibility. Ask yourself if there's a downside to publishing your book. Is there? And is there an upside to *not* finishing it? Ask these questions and notice what comes up. This will most likely be one of the fears that are addressed in this book. Look up the corresponding chapter to move through this fear.

If your book actually sucks, that's not the end of the world either. It only means that your book needs extra love, attention, and work. That's all. It does NOT mean that *you* suck or that there's something wrong with *you*. Shift into curiosity and explore what exactly is "off" with your book. What needs to change to improve it? What will make your book good enough to publish? Change what needs changing and keep moving forward. If you're not sure what needs to change, talk it through with your coach, a colleague, your editor or a friend. Whatever your book needs, you can handle it!!

WHAT TO DO WHEN YOU HAVE NO INSPIRATION

Here are several things you can do when this happens.

Tip One: Write through it

Take out your journal and write about not having any inspiration. What do you think this means? How does it feel? What would you write if you felt inspired? That may sound like a weird question, but answer it anyway. You never know what will come up. Write down all your answers.

Tip Two: Think through it

What is it you want to say *exactly*? What point do you want to make? What do you want your reader to take away from a specific chapter? What are one to three main points that chapter needs to address?

Tip Three: Do some creative writing

Write something completely different. Here are some creative prompts to play with.

Ask a friend to give you three to five random words. Write a poem or short story using these words.

Take a random book from your bookshelf, open it with your eyes closed and put your finger on a page, without looking. The sentence your finger lands on is the first sentence of a short story.

Pick a random word. Set an alarm for five minutes. Write about this word until the alarm goes off. Do not think about it!! Your writing doesn't have to be pretty, and it doesn't have to be a story or poem. This is about letting the words flow through you and out of you. About getting out of the way and letting inspiration take over. **You always have access to words and thoughts. The more you practice getting out of the way and letting your muse take over, the easier it becomes to write.** Part Two *Chapter 8: Get Out of Your Way* shows you how to step aside and let the words come through.

CHAPTER 15

WRITER'S BLOCK

I don't believe in writer's block. You can *feel* stuck, but you never really *are*. There's always a reason you feel blocked. And there's always a solution. Believe me, I know. I discovered many solutions in the nine years it took to write and publish *Unmute Your Life*. I've felt stuck dozens of times during those years for all the reasons below. Read through them to see which one catches your eye. That's most likely what's going on for you now.

Reason One: Self-doubt

You can do several things when you doubt yourself. Pick the suggestion that speaks to you most.

- Remind yourself that self-doubt is part of the creative cycle. Read Part Two *Chapter 7: The Creative Cycle* again.
- Make a list of fifteen (or more) reasons you *can* publish your book.
- Make a list of at least ten reasons it makes perfect sense that you're the right person to write about your topic.
- Make a list of at least fifteen times you doubted that you could do something, but you succeeded anyway. Seeing this list restores your self-confidence.

Reason Two: Self-criticism

Use one of the solutions above. What also helps is to be kind, gentle, loving, and mild to yourself. How would you treat someone you love if they tell you they have writer's block? Treat yourself that way. Tell yourself what you would tell them.

Reason Three: Comparing yourself or your book to others

Bring your focus back to yourself. Remind yourself why there's space for your book. Go back to the beginning of Part Four and read *Chapter 2: The Fear That No One Is Waiting for Your Book* again.

Reason Four: Feeling anxious or overwhelmed

Bring your attention back to this present moment. Worries are always about something that already happened (the past) or something that hasn't happened yet (the future). In this moment, you are okay. In this moment, all is well. Read Part Two *Chapter 8: Get Out of Your Way* again for more tips.

Focus on the task at hand. Forget about everything else. Give this moment and your current activity your full attention. Give the next moment your full attention after that.

Make a to-do list. Sometimes you lose the overview of what needs to happen, which can trigger overwhelm. Once you're clear on what needs to be done, you can relax again.

Talk it through with a friend or your coach.

Reason Five: Fear

Explore what you fear and find tips to deal with it in one of these chapters. Or work with one of the following general solutions.

- Focus on why writing this book matters to you. Why do you want to publish it? This makes your dream bigger than your fear—a surefire way to move forward even when you're scared.

- Be loving and gentle with yourself. Love the part of you that's scared.
- Remind yourself that fear is part of the creative cycle, too. It will pass!
- Remind yourself that fear has no more power over you than you give it. Fears are only thoughts in your mind.

Reason Six: You need a break

Give yourself time to pause. Relaxing, focusing on something else, and getting rest are part of ALL creative activities, including writing a book!

Reason Seven: Ideas need to percolate

Sometimes your ideas need time to ripen and grow. You know there's something you want to express, but you can't grasp the words yet. They're just outside your reach. Let them brew and percolate. It will improve your book! You'll know when your idea has grown enough to be birthed: you'll feel like writing again and the words will flow out with ease.

Reason Eight: Something else needs your attention first

Maybe you need to work on another book-related task. Maybe something completely different calls for your attention, like clearing out your attic or doing your taxes. Whatever it is, you need to handle it before you write.

Be mindful of the difference between something that *really* needs your attention and procrastination. How do you know the difference? By being super honest with yourself. Do you *really* need to do this or are you avoiding to work on your book?

General solutions

Write something else. Words are *always* available to you. Write a blog or a social media update. Write a poem or write in your journal. Write about your writer's block. Write about how you feel and what you think about feeling stuck. Get all the thoughts and inner unrest out of your system.

Another solution is to move your body. Do yoga, take a walk, go for a run, do a workout, or dance. When your body moves, your energy flows, too. Sometimes that's enough to help you get unstuck. Physical exercise also gets you out of your head, which can bring you the mental space you need to receive fresh ideas and inspiration.

What you experience as writer's block can last a minute, an hour, a day or longer. Don't get hung up on how long it lasts. Don't push it away. What you resist persists. Explore what's happening underneath. What's the real issue? Address that. Before you know it, you're back in flow again.

GENERAL EXERCISES TO DEAL WITH FEAR

Throughout the book you've already received several tips on dealing with fears and doubts. But maybe you need more. For that reason, I'm sharing some general exercises on dealing with fear. They're a small collection of exercises from my book *Unmute Your Life - break free from fear & go for what you REALLY want.*

Exercise One: Work with your breath

Your breath is a wonderful instrument that can help calm you down in a matter of minutes. It's physically impossible to breathe deep in your belly AND feel anxious or stressed at the same time. Your breath is either deep and you're calm, OR your breath is shallow and you're not (or less) calm. This means that all you have to do to relax is breath deeper and slower. You can do that in the following ways.

Breathe deeper into your belly. Put one hand underneath your navel and feel your belly rise and fall with each breath. Keep breathing deeply and slowly until you feel calm again.

OR

Exhale completely using the muscles in your belly to push the last bit of breath out. You'll notice that your lungs will automatically fill up. Exhale completely, push all the air out, and let the inhalation happen naturally. Repeat until you feel calm.

OR

Breathe in for four counts, pause for four counts, breathe out for four counts. Repeat until you feel calm.

Exercise Two: Your fear is the portal to liberation and gold

Your fears are treasure keepers. They're a portal to your next breakthrough and growth. There's ALWAYS gold at the other end of it. By looking for the reward upfront, your fear not only becomes smaller, but it also becomes something you *want* to move through. You can get there by asking yourself questions like these.

- What becomes possible for me when I move through this fear?
- What becomes possible for my clients?
- What becomes possible for my business?
- What becomes possible for my children, partner, or family?
- What becomes possible for my friends and community?
- What do I gain by moving through this fear?
- What do I NEVER have to put up with ever again when I move through this fear?
- What do I win by moving forward?
- What else can I do once I have moved through this fear?
- How else will I benefit when I move through this fear?
- What is waiting for me at the other end of it?
- What freedom, liberation, and joy are waiting for me on the other end?
- What will heal when I move through this fear?
- What transformation becomes possible for me as a result of moving through it?

These questions help you focus on your dreams more than on your fears. And it becomes easier to take another step forward.

Exercise Three: Cultivate your excitement

When you're enthusiastic enough, your fear can no longer stop you. So tap into your curiosity and enhance your excitement by answering these questions.

- How cool would it be to see your dream unfold?
- How amazing would it be to live your dreams?
- How will you feel when you move through this fear and do the things that call you?

I hope these exercises help you move through fears and doubts if they come up. The most important thing to remember, however, is to keep focusing on your DREAM instead of on your FEAR. Bring your attention back to what you stand to gain when you publish your book instead of what you fear you might lose. Keep looking at what's right instead of at what's wrong. Remind yourself that things may work out well instead of thinking about what might go wrong. Remind yourself why writing your book matters to you. Remind yourself how publishing your book will transform yourself, your business, your readers, and potentially the world. Read through your answers and the intention you created in Part One. How is writing your book better than *not* writing it? How will it feel to hold your book in your hands? Keep bringing your attention back to these feelings and dreams. And keep going until your book is done. You got this!

WHEN YOUR FIRST DRAFT IS FINISHED

Writing your first draft is the first phase of publishing your book. A BIG phase! And definitely the most important one. That's why I focus on writing your first draft in this book.

There are other steps to take after that. You can find them below so you know what else you need to do to publish your book.

Step One: Editing

First, self-edit your book until you can't improve it further. Here's how I self-edit in a nutshell:

After I finish my first draft, I let the manuscript rest for a couple of weeks. At least three weeks and eight at most. This allows me to read my work with fresh eyes. Then, I read the entire book in one go *without editing or changing anything*. I only make notes: does the book feel complete? What looks good? What needs to change? Does the order of the chapters make sense?

After that first read-through, I start to edit. I go over each chapter and start polishing, rewriting, adding and deleting examples, sentences or even entire chapters. I change the order of the chapters if necessary.

Once the book feels complete and almost done, I number the chapters and create the table of contents. I run the document through a spellchecker and correct typos and spelling and grammar mistakes.

Finally, I print the document and go over it with a fine-tooth comb one last time. I make the last changes and send the manuscript to my editor. By this time I've gone over the book at least seven times myself. Going over it more often is pointless now, because I can't see my own blind spots. It's time for a trained professional to take over.

Hand your manuscript over to an editor next. This elevates your book and improves it in ways you couldn't have done on your own.

Step Two: Design

Hire a professional to design your cover. Don't do it yourself. It needs to look professional. People really judge a book by its cover! It's the first thing people see, so make sure it looks good.

I also hire a professional to design the interior of the paperback and format the e-book. These are not my skillsets, and I'm not interested in learning how it works. I choose to delegate everything I don't like to do or what I'm not good at.

Some people choose to do it themselves. You can, of course, but ONLY do that if the result looks good! Why would you put in so much effort, time, and energy into writing a book only to end up with a sloppy or unprofessional-looking result?

Step Three: Publishing

There are many ways to self-publish your book. You could also try the traditional route of finding a publisher for your book, of course.

I have experience with both and prefer self-publishing. When I self-published my first book in 2008, print on demand (POD) was not really a thing, at least, not in The Netherlands. Self-publishing your book meant printing your book at a local printer, stacking your shed with them, and handling the distribution yourself. This was fun for a while but quickly became a hassle. That's why I contacted a publisher, so they could take over the sales and distribution and save me a ton of time. I was thrilled and grateful when they published my book. I LOVED it!

Still, I went back to self-publishing. Why? Because a traditional publisher doesn't add much and costs you freedom. Yes, they arrange for someone to design the cover and edit your book. Yes, they put it on their website and maybe do a bit of marketing. (They only pull out all the stops for big names or people with a massive platform).

But you don't have 100% freedom. They have a say in your cover and editorial choices. You still have to write the book yourself and DO ALL THE MARKETING AND PUBLICITY YOURSELF!

For *all* that work, you only receive a tiny percentage of the proceeds. Even when you sell a lot of books, you make little money because of the super-small percentage you receive. (I received 8% royalties for the first five thousand copies, and 10% on all copies after that. That's pretty standard if you're a writer no one has heard of yet.)

It's not difficult to find a designer for your cover. It's not difficult to find a good editor. Yes, you pay for it yourself, but you'll make it back with the MUCH higher royalties you receive when you self-publish. For me, having 100% freedom to do whatever I want with my books is the main reason I choose self-publishing over traditional publishing. That's why I went back to it. It's the best choice for me, but for you traditional publishing might be better.

Step Four: Marketing and promotion

Publishing your book does not automatically lead to sales. You have to promote and market your book, too. If you already have a business, you know how this works. If marketing is completely new to you, don't worry, you can learn everything you need to know! You can send press releases, pitch your book to podcasts or magazines, and use social media to talk about your book. If you do an internet search for "book marketing," you'll find lots of other tips. Choose advice that resonates with you and ignore the rest. There are no strict rules you need to follow, and there are as many ways to promote a book as there are authors.

If you need more information on these topics, everything you need to know is just a click away. There's plenty of excellent information available! For now, focus on finishing your first draft, though. That's what's most important. You'll figure out the other steps along the way just like I did!****

**** Don't want to figure it out on your own? Check out my online program *Write Your Non-Fiction Book in 3 Months (in only 30 minutes per day)* That might be just what you need. You can read all about it on www.3monthbook.com

WHAT'S NEXT?

I hope this book helped you write your first draft. If you've already finished it, congratulations!! Writing your book is a big and exciting deal. You've reached a milestone most people never reach. Yay, you!!!

If you're looking for more inspiration or support, I've got you covered.

First, you can get complimentary gifts, which include examples of book structures, an overview of what to put in your book, and how I go from an outline to writing here: www.bookfreebees.com

If you'd like to learn the other steps to self-publish your book, check out my online program Write Your Book in 3 Months (in only 30 minutes per day) here: www.3monthbook.com

And come say hi on social media! You can find me here:

Instagram: www.instagram.com/brigitte_van_tuijl/
Facebook: www.facebook.com/brigittevantuijl.artofdivineselfishness/
Twitter: www.twitter.com/brigittevanT

Thank you for reading this book. I hope you enjoyed it and if so, please leave me a brilliant review! Or just a nice one. That'll make me happy, too. :-)

For now, I wish you all the best, and good luck with your book!

Love,
Brigitte

OTHER BOOKS BY BRIGITTE

The Gap - bridge the space between where you are and where you want to be
No matter how big your dream or goal is, realizing it can be easier than you think. This book shows you how.

The Inner Minimalist - clear the clutter of your mind for a simpler, quieter and happier life
This book helps you clear your mind for more (inner) freedom and happiness!

The Art of Divine Selfishness Series
Book One: Unmute Your Life - break free from fear & go for what you REALLY want
This book helps you uncover your TRUE dreams and make them real.

Book Two: The Art of Divine Selfishness - transform your life, your business & the world by putting YOU first
If you want to create a business and life you adore, you need to put yourself first! This book shows you how.

Books in Dutch
Ontdek Wat Je Écht Wilt En Maak Daar (Je) Werk Van
Een praktisch en inspirerend werkboek om zelfstandig in kaart te brengen wat je écht wilt – en daar je werk van te maken.

You can find more information on these and upcoming books at www.booksbybrigitte.com